D0746693

Feeding the Roots of Self-Expression and Freedom

Feeding the Roots of Self-Expression and Freedom

Jimmy Santiago Baca
with Kym Sheehan and Denise VanBriggle

Foreword by Rex L. Veeder
Afterword by Diane Torres-Velásquez

TEACHERS COLLEGE PRESS

TEACHERS COLLEGE | COLUMBIA UNIVERSITY

NEW YORK AND LONDON

Published by Teachers College Press, 1234 Amsterdam Avenue, New York, NY 10027

Cover design by Charles Rue Woods.
Cover photograph of trees by enterphoto / iStock by Getty Images.
Photo credits can be found on page 127

Library of Congress Cataloging-in-Publication Data is available at loc.gov

ISBN 978-0-8077-5955-4 (paper)
ISBN 978-0-8077-7743-5 (ebook)

Printed on acid-free paper
Manufactured in the United States of America

26   25   24   23   22   21   20   19   8   7   6   5   4   3   2   1

Contents

Illuminating Outward

Rehumanization Process

to **Gabe Baca**,

this book would have never happened had he
not digitized all the writings and presented the idea

Foreword

I began teaching writing, speech, and literature in 1970. I was fortunate to have met Jimmy Baca in the later 70s through his writing and our letters—at a time when he was emerging from being a convict into being convinced by words, images, stories, and felt thoughts that he had a power to transform himself and others for the better. He was a poet because he had to be. The words made him do it.

We are convicted by things other than the law—we can have conviction in life. We become aware of Jimmy Baca's message and feel his thoughts. There is for writers, magic in words where a convict can gain the conviction to choose life and a place to stand. We find in Jimmy Baca's words and felt thoughts a reason for acting on the world.

Almost every aspect of prison life has its analogies in the lives of those who are defined as "at risk" in our education system. Where the one experiences being in a prison cell, the other is confined by the physical limitations of poverty or the judgments of officials who see them as inferior students. The sheer number of at-risk students is overwhelming. Once, as an administrator for a community and technical college, I noted that every student who enrolled was classified by the standard definitions as *at risk*.

Is it any wonder that the student and the prisoner should feel a strong connection? And, is it any wonder that at-risk students are prisoners in training, where school systems can and often do become drilling grounds for incarceration? This *seasoning* for a life of incarceration begins in elementary school and continues until the student is done with education and happy to ignore the pleas of teachers to be a life-long learner.

The word *seasoning* has a history that I want to call upon to help explain *A Place to Stand,* Baca's documentary and book, and this book that puts the meanings we find or create in *A Place to Stand* into personal and even passionate clarity.

Like the prisoner, like the at-risk student, we are made to endure a journey through life that prepares us for inhumanity and servitude. This was, in fact, the reason for the hard crossing and the incarceration of Africans or the horror endured by those incarcerated by the Nazis. The overseer, the master, was charged by a system to break Africans and Jews in order to force them to accept their condition as slaves or as inferior human beings who deserved to die or be worked to death—to be owned, to be used, to be slaughtered.

In this sense, the book and documentary persuade us that overwhelming cruelty can be turned to a generous humanity. Once we believe this we must ask ourselves, since we now know something powerful about life, prison, and prisoners, *what difference does it make to the way we think, feel, and act?* For the writers of this book, the answer is to offer ways of moving from being seasoned to becoming free.

There are countless ways to have our humanity challenged in life. It is not necessary to be a convict to identify what is taken from us by systems and individuals who profit from our being less human and more and more something to use—to buy. When we become determined to resist being bought and sold, then we wonder what to do and how to make a difference in our own lives and the lives of others. This, I believe, is the movement in *A Place to Stand* and the reason for the first part of this book. If we recognize how our circumstances have seasoned and dehumanized us.

How is it we can move toward being free? How does being engaged with *A Place to Stand* and this book help us find our own place to stand in the world? If through writing and the arts we engage in acting imaginatively, reflecting, and thinking carefully about our circumstances, with empathy toward other human beings, are we endangering ourselves? Should we be happy in ignorance and strong in unexamined judgments?

These are questions a writer and reader will have to answer in response to the documentary, the poems, and the prompts that follow. If someone goes through the fire and ice of examining her or his life and the lives of others in this way, I believe he or she is moving toward freedom and away from being dehumanized. This book offers a way, a path, to follow the road to freedom from despair.

Are you willing to take that journey? Be brave. Be resolute. Be a resistance fighter for your freedom and the freedom of others. If you will do the work here offered, you will be these things, and the world will look different because you will have made it different.

Dr. Rex Veeder, Professor of English,
St. Cloud University, St. Cloud, Minnesota

Acknowledgments

First and foremost, there would be no book without the writings of Jimmy Santiago Baca or without his trust in the co-authors to share his life's struggle. His faith in the co-authors' ability to understand the importance of each piece of paper is brought together within the text. Jimmy's gift of knowing when individual journeys require interaction from others is uncanny and almost always correct.

Additionally, his son, Gabriel Baca, was the one who unearthed these poetic treasures at the Stanford archives in 2010. He and his colleague, Daniel Glick, were searching the archives for information for the documentary film on Jimmy's life and found boxes and boxes of never published poems. He culled these poems from those resources.

The cover art of Charles Rue Woods captured the essence of this work in so many ways. Our collective gratitude for his perceptions and masterful graphic art is immense. This vision is our collective image.

Kym Sheehan and Denise VanBriggle on
Feeding Our Own Roots of
Freedom & Self-Expression

We (Kym and Denise) often marvel at Jimmy Santiago Baca's (JSB) ability to intuit just the right combination of people to connect to just the right project. Neither of us had met the other when Jimmy tossed us together in November 2011. The common denominators? Jimmy had visited both of our school systems between 2009 and 2011. We shared an appreciation for his poetry and prose and a deep affection for Jimmy as a person. We both said "YES" to the project without a moment's hesitation. Well-meaning friends and family encouraged us "to get something in writing" and "not to give our professional services away," yet we listened to our hearts.

Since one of us (Kym) lives in Florida and the other (Denise) in Pennsylvania, we connected via Skype for the first five months of our collaboration. In March of 2012 during Denise's vacation to Florida, we spent one intensive day brainstorming, writing, and revising in a funky coffee shop, Ginny and Jane E's, located on Anna Maria Island.

After that face-to-face visit, we resumed our Skype sessions to shepherd the project to completion. Throughout our time together, we have developed a treasured friendship and discovered a host of uncanny similarities along the way, most of which Jimmy could not have known when he invited us to work on this project with him.

- We entered education after having successful careers in other arenas.
- We taught school for many years.
- We became champions of literacy along the way.
- We became National Writing Project Fellows.
- We became professional developers during our careers.
- We presented at National Council of Teachers of English and National Writing Project conferences.
- We assumed leadership roles at the local, state, and national levels.

- We served as fund-raisers for the documentary film project, *A Place to Stand,* chronicling the life of Jimmy Santiago Baca as reflected within his highly acclaimed memoir of the same title.
- We possess an understanding of prison systems from a variety of perspectives.
- We practice yoga and believe in the mind-body-spirit connection.
- We appreciate art, history, antiquities, and music.
- We believe everyone should follow their heart's desire.
- We believe everyone matters and has a story to tell.
- We believe self-expression in any form holds the power to heal and the potential to free us from real or imaginary chains that bind us.

This book would not exist without the constant encouragement of our friends and families. You hold in your hands our labor of love.

~ Denise and Kym

Readers unfamiliar with JSB's memoir *A Place to Stand* (2001) may find the following essay from *Working in the Dark* (1992) especially useful in foregrounding the collection of unpublished prison poems to follow.

Coming Into Language
Jimmy Santiago Baca

On weekend graveyard shifts at St. Joseph's Hospital, I worked the emergency room, mopping up pools of blood and carting plastic bags stuffed with arms, legs, and hands to the outdoor incinerator. I enjoyed the quiet, away from the screams of shot-gunned, knifed, and mangled kids writhing on gurneys outside the operating rooms. Ambulance sirens shrieked and squad car lights reddened the cool nights, flashing against the hospital walls: gray-red, gray-red. On slow nights I would lock the door of the administration office, search the reference library for a book on female anatomy, and with my feet propped on the desk, leaf through the illustrations, smoking my cigarette. I was seventeen.

One night my eye was caught by a familiar-looking word on the spine of a book, the title was *450 Years of Chicano History in Pictures*. On the cover were black-and-white photos: Padre Hidalgo exhorting Mexican peasants to revolt against the Spanish dictators; Anglo vigilantes hanging two Mexicans from a tree; a young Mexican woman with rifle and ammunition belts crisscrossing her breast; César Chavez and field workers marching for fair wages; Chicano railroad workers laying creosote ties; Chicanas laboring at machines in textile factories; and Chicanas picketing and hoisting boycott signs.

From the time I was seven, teachers had been punishing me for not knowing my lessons by making me stick my nose in a circle chalked on the blackboard. Ashamed of not understanding and fearful of asking questions, I dropped out of school in the ninth grade. At seventeen I still didn't know how to read, but those pictures confirmed my identity. I stole the book that night, stashing it for safety under the slop-sink until I got off work. Back at my boardinghouse, I showed the book to friends. All of us were amazed; this book told us we were alive. We, too, had defended ourselves with our fists against hostile Anglos, gasping for breath in fights with the policemen who outnumbered us. The book reflected back to us our struggle in a way that made us proud.

Most of my life I felt like a target in the cross hairs of a hunter's rifle. When strangers and outsiders questioned me I felt the hang-rope tighten around my neck and the trapdoor creak beneath my feet. There was nothing as humiliating as being unable to express myself, and my inarticulateness increased my sense of jeopardy, of being endangered. I felt intimidated and vulnerable, ridiculed and scorned. Behind a mask of humility, I seethed with mute rebellion.

Before I was eighteen, I was arrested on suspicion of murder after refusing to explain a deep cut on my forearm. With shocking speed I found myself handcuffed to a chain gang of inmates and bused to a holding facility to await trial. There I met men, prisoners, who read aloud to each other the works of Neruda, Paz, Sabines, Nemerov, and Hemingway. Never had I felt such freedom as in that dormitory. Listening to the words of these writers, I felt that invisible threat from without lessen—my sense of teetering on a rotting plank over swamp water where famished alligators clapped their horny snouts for my blood. While I listened to the words of the poets, the alligators slumbered powerless in their lairs. Their language was the magic that could liberate me from myself, transform me into another person, and transport me to other places far away.

And when they closed the books, these Chicanos, and went into their own Chicano language, they made barrio life come alive for me in the fullness of its vitality. I began to learn my own language, the bilingual words and phrases explaining to me my place in the universe. Every day I felt like the paper boy taking delivery of the latest news of the day.

Months later I was released, as I had suspected I would be. I had been guilty of nothing but shattering the windshield of my girlfriend's car in a fit of rage.

Two years passed. I was twenty now, and behind bars again. The federal marshals had failed to provide convincing evidence to extradite me to Arizona on a drug charge, but still I was being held. They had ninety days to prove I was guilty. The only evidence against me was that my girlfriend had been at the scene of the crime with my driver's license in her purse. They had to come up with something else. But there was nothing else. Eventually they negotiated a deal with the actual drug dealer, who took the stand against me. When the judge hit me with a million-dollar bail, I emptied my pockets on his booking desk: twenty-six cents.

One night in my third month in the county jail, I was mopping the floor in front of the booking desk. Some detectives had kneed an old drunk and handcuffed him to the booking bars. His shrill screams raked my nerves like a hacksaw on bone, the desperate protest of his dignity against their inhumanity. But the detectives just laughed as he tried to rise and kicked him to his knees. When they went to the bathroom to pee and the desk attendant walked to the file cabinet to pull the arrest record, I shot my arm through the bars, grabbed one of the attendant's university textbooks, and tucked it in my overalls. It was the only way I had of protesting.

It was late when I returned to my cell. Under my blanket I switched on a pen flashlight and opened the thick book at random, scanning the pages. I could hear the jailer making his rounds on the other tiers. The jangle of his keys and the sharp click of his boot heels intensified my solitude. Slowly I enunciated the words . . . p-o-n-d, ripple. It scared me that I had been reduced to this to find comfort. I always had thought reading a waste of time, that nothing could be gained by it. Only by action, by moving out into the world and confronting and challenging the obstacles, could one learn anything worth knowing.

Even as I tried to convince myself that I was merely curious, I became so absorbed in how the sounds created music in me and happiness, I forgot where I was. Memories began to quiver in me, glowing with a strange but familiar intimacy in which I found refuge. For a while, a deep sadness overcame me, as if I had chanced on a long-lost friend and mourned the years of separation. But soon the heartache of having missed so much of life, that had numbed me since I was a child, gave way, as if a grave illness lifted itself from me and I was cured, innocently believing in the beauty of life again. I stumblingly repeated the author's name as I fell asleep, saying it *over* and over in the dark: Words-worth, Words-worth.

Before long my sister came to visit me, and I joked about taking her to a place called Kubla Khan and getting her a blind date with this *vato* named Coleridge who lived on the seacoast and was on morphine. When I asked her to make a trip into enemy territory to buy me a grammar book, she said she couldn't. Bookstores intimidated her, because she, too, could neither read nor write.

Days later, with a stub pencil I whittled sharp with my teeth, I propped a Red Chief notebook on my knees and wrote my first words. From that moment, a hunger for poetry possessed me.

Until then, I had felt as if I had been born into a raging ocean where I swam relentlessly, flailing my arms in hope of rescue, of reaching a shoreline I never sighted. Never solid ground beneath me, never a resting place. I had lived with only the desperate hope to stay afloat; that and nothing more.

But when at last I wrote my first words on the page, I felt an island rising beneath my feet like the back of a whale. As more and more words emerged, I could finally rest: I had a place to stand for the first time in my life. The island grew, with each page, into a continent inhabited by people I knew and mapped with the life I lived.

I wrote about it all—about people I had loved or hated, about the brutalities and ecstasies of my life. And, for the first time, the child in me who had witnessed and endured unspeakable terrors cried out not just in impotent despair, but with the power of language. Suddenly, through language, through writing, my grief and my joy could be shared with anyone who would listen. And I could do this all alone; I could do it anywhere. I was no longer a captive of demons eating away at me, no longer a victim of other people's mockery and loathing, that had made me clench my fist white with rage and grit my teeth to silence. Words now pleaded back with the bleak lucidity of hurt. They were wrong, those others, and now I could say it.

Through language I was free. I could respond, escape, indulge; embrace or reject earth or the cosmos. I was launched on an endless journey without boundaries or rules, in which I could salvage the floating fragments of my past, or be born anew in the spontaneous ignition of understanding some heretofore concealed aspect of myself. Each word steamed with the hot lava juices of my primordial making, and I crawled out of stanzas dripping with birth-blood, reborn and freed from the chaos of my life. The child in the dark room of my heart, that had never been able to find or reach the light switch, flicked it on now; and I found in the room a stranger, myself, who had waited so many years to speak again. My words struck in me lightning crackles of elation and thunderhead storms of grief.

When I had been in the county jail longer than anyone else, I was made a trustee. One morning, after a fist fight, I went to the unlocked and unoccupied office used for lawyer-client meetings, to think. The bare white room with its fluorescent tube lighting seemed to expose and illuminate my dark and worthless life. And yet, for the first time, I had something to lose—my chance to read, to write; a way to live with dignity and meaning, that had opened for me when I stole that scuffed, second-hand book about the Romantic poets. In prison, the abscess had been lanced.

"I will never do any work in this prison system as long as I am not allowed to get my G.E.D." That's what I told the reclassification panel. The captain flicked off the tape recorder. He looked at me hard and said, 'You'll never walk outta here alive. Oh, you'll work, put a copper penny on that, you'll work."

After that interview I was confined to deadlock maximum security in a subterranean dungeon, with ground-level chicken-wired windows painted gray. Twenty-three hours a day I was in that cell. I kept sane by borrowing books from the other cons on the tier. Then, just before Christmas, I received a letter from Harry, a charity house Samaritan who doled out hot soup to the homeless in Phoenix. He had picked my name from a list of cons who had no one to write to them. I wrote back asking for a grammar book, and a week later received one of Mary Baker Eddy's treatises on salvation and redemption, with Spanish and English on opposing pages. Pacing my cell all day and most of each night, I grappled with grammar until I was able to write a long true-romance confession for a con to send to his pen pal. He paid me with a pack of smokes. Soon I had a thriving barter business, exchanging my poems and letters for novels, commissary pencils, and writing tablets.

One day I tore two flaps from the cardboard box that held all my belongings and punctured holes along the edge of each flap and along the border of a ream of state-issue paper. After I had aligned them to form a spine, I threaded the holes with a shoestring, and sketched on the cover a hummingbird fluttering above a rose. This was my first journal.

Whole afternoons I wrote, unconscious of passing time or whether it was day or night. Sunbursts exploded from the lead tip of my pencil, words that grafted me into awareness of who I was; peeled back to a burning core of bleak terror, an embryo floating in the image of water, I cracked out of the shell wide-eyed and insane. Trees grew out of the palms of my hands, the threatening otherness of life dissolved, and I became one with the air and sky, the dirt and the iron and concrete. There was no longer any distinction between the other and I. Language made bridges of fire between me and I saw. I entered into the blade of grass, the basketball, the con's eye and child's soul.

At night I flew. I conversed with floating heads in my cell, and visited strange houses where lonely women brewed tea and rocked in wicker rocking chairs listening to sad Joni Mitchell songs.

Before long I was frayed like a rope carrying too much weight, that suddenly snaps. I quit talking. Bars, walls, steel bunk and floor bristled with millions of poem-making sparks. My face was no longer familiar to me. The only reality was the swirling cornucopia of images in my mind, the voices in the air. Mid-air a cactus blossom would appear, a snake flame in blinding dance around it, stunning me like a guard's fist striking my neck from behind.

The prison administrators tried several tactics to get me to work. For six months, after the next monthly prison review, they sent cons to my cell to hassle me. When the guard would open my cell door to let one of them in, I'd leap out and fight him and get sent to thirty-day isolation. I did a lot of isolation time. But I honed my image-making talents in that sensory-deprived solitude. Finally they moved me to death row, and after that to "nut-run," the tier that housed the mentally disturbed.

As the months passed, I became more and more sluggish. My eyelids were heavy, I could no longer write or read, and I slept all the time.

One day a guard took me out to the exercise field. For the first time in years I felt grass and earth under my feet. It was spring. The sun warmed my face as I sat on the bleachers watching the cons box and run, hit the handball, lift weights. Some of them stopped to ask how I was, but I found it impossible to utter a syllable. My tongue would not move, saliva drooled from the corners of my mouth. I had been so heavily medicated I could not summon the slightest gesture. Yet inside me a small voice cried out, I am fine! I am hurt now but I will come back! I am fine!

Back in my cell, for weeks I refused to eat. Styrofoam cups of urine and hot water were hurled at me. Other things happened. There were beatings, shock therapy, and intimidation. Later, I regained some clarity of mind, but there was a place in my heart where I had died. My life had compressed itself into an unbearable dread of being. The strain had been too much. I had stepped over that line where a human being has lost more than he can bear, where the pain is too intense, and he knows he is changed forever. I was now capable of killing, coldly and without feeling. I was empty, as I have never, before or since, known emptiness. I had no connection to this life.

But then, the encroaching darkness that began to envelop me forced me to re-form and give birth to myself again in the chaos. I withdrew even deeper into the world of language, cleaving the diamonds of verbs and nouns, plunging into the brilliant light of poetry's regenerative mystery. Words gave off rings of white energy, radar signals from powers beyond me that infused me with truth. I believed what I wrote, because I wrote what was true. My words did not come from books or textual formulas, but from a deep faith in the voice of my heart.

I had been steeped in self-loathing and rejected by everyone and every-thing—society, family, cons, God and demons. But now I had become as the burning ember floating in darkness that descends on a dry leaf and sets flame to forests. The word was the ember and the forest was my life.

I was born a poet one noon, gazing at weeds and creosoted grass at the base of a telephone pole outside my grilled cell window. The words I wrote then sailed me out of myself, and I was transported and metamorphosed into the images they made. From the dirty brown blades of grass came bolts of electrical light that jolted loose my old self; through the top of my head that self was released and reshaped in the clump of scrawny grass. Through language I became the grass, speaking its language and feeling its green feelings and black root sensations. Earth was my mother and I bathed in sunshine. Minuscule speckles of sunlight passed through my green skin and metabolized in my blood.

Writing bridged my divided life of prisoner and free man. I wrote of the emotional butchery of prisons, and of my acute gratitude for poetry. Where my blind doubt and spontaneous trust in life met, I discovered empathy and compassion. The power to express myself was a welcome storm rasping at tendril roots, flooding my soul's cracked dirt. Writing was water that cleansed the wound and fed the parched root of my heart.

I wrote to sublimate my rage, from a place where all hope is gone, from a madness of having been damaged too much, from a silence of killing rage. I wrote to avenge the betrayals of a lifetime, to purge the bitterness of injustice. I wrote with a deep groan of doom in my blood, bewildered and dumbstruck, from an indestructible love of life, to affirm breath and laughter and the abiding innocence of things. I wrote the way I wept, and danced, and made love.

Making the Rounds

Jimmy Santiago Baca

Most poetry textbooks or guides for teachers focus on the elements of the craft; they describe in detail the workings of metaphors, rhyme schemes, and various aspects of poetic traditions. This, of course, is a must for any teacher of the art. But how can teachers conduct workshops for "bored kids"? How can teachers turn problem classes—every instructor's fear—into memorably beautiful ones?

Kids don't need to be taught the essence of poetry. No matter whether they are in a rez schoolroom, a Hopi hogan, or a prestigious private school such as Exeter in New Hampshire, Oregon, or the hardcore but beautiful barrios of San Jose—they understand the language of childhood.

What follows are some illustrations of my experiences with students, beginning with my experiences in prison. Though they live in adult bodies, prisoners are often emotional children—psychically damaged emotional amputees, unglamorous kids who've committed crimes not only against society but also against themselves.

1.

My teaching "career" started when, as an inmate, I visited other convicts' cells. I sat on the concrete with the bars between us, reading them poetry. I'm not sure why poetry was so popular with prisoners, but I have a guess. Many had no books in their homes growing up, yet often family members had memorized poems—Spanish speakers call those dichos, pithy sayings that give a lot of meaning for the few words the sentence uses. Mothers nursed their babies and hummed poetry to them, and when the children grew older, their mothers whispered bandit epics into their little ten-year-old ears. Those epics inspired them to want to become gangsters—in other words, to live flamboyant lives with drama and conflict. Too often, though, these lives were cut short.

2.

I was released from prison in 1979. After having had a couple of poetry books published, I started teaching elementary school students through the New Mexico Arts Division (funded by the National Endowment for the Arts). My students reintroduced me to the imaginative language of childhood—the speech that carries the excitement of images, the fires of unpredictable vocabulary, the surprise word choices reeling with hilarious giants and talking ants and Santa Clauses who are not Nordic or Caucasian but Chicano and who burrow beyond San Felipe Pueblo deep into the nearby Sandia Mountains outside Albuquerque. A Santa Claus who has, instead of reindeer a herd of mules he dresses up like reindeer for Christmas and who even likes tortillas, tacos y burritos, and beans and chili. When the instructor opens up to this type of imaginative language, the conversation about poetry with children becomes an adventure. But this adventure must first refer directly to kids' day-to-day experiences—that is essential.

3.

If we turn to a slightly older age group—adolescents, say, in a classroom for students at risk—we find some students who don't like school, will not study, refuse to collaborate with the teacher, and disregard lessons and curricula as if homework were a terminal disease. At this point, as a poet-teacher I know that I need to surprise them. How can I do this? What teaching tools can help me shake them into wakefulness?

Here is one example: I once asked violent students at a charter high school to consider a poem that asked for forgiveness for beating on poor people, for clubbing down Mexicans in the street for no good reason other than that it was entertaining. All the kids in the room got it, nodded their heads in assent, hung their heads low, and motioned with facial expressions that they appreciated the poem. They knew a woman had written it, and they wondered why. Why did she need forgiveness from them? That's when the author—whom I had invited to the class— explained that she had been a police officer in San Diego for twelve years and had routinely beaten Mexicans for no reason. All the students were stunned, unsure how to react. A cop apologizing to them? No way. An ex-cop writing poetry? No way. Every student's mouth was agape. Their perspective on life was suddenly realigned. Bravo for poetry. The students felt more human after an ex-cop had apologized to them and written a forgiveness poem for them—and after they had accepted it.

Of course, it is not every day that one can bring an ex-cop to recite poetry to an inner-city high school audience. But the point here is simple: the work must connect to the audience's everyday experience, cast a spell on the audience, and teach a lesson—something worth holding on to.

4.

We now fly from the Southwest to South Florida, where I'm teaching poetry to a class of middle-school kids. I have a list of themes (from my textbook for teachers and students, *Stories from the Edge*) that I want them to tackle. Among the mostly fun themes is a hard one: write about a painful experience. On this occasion, everyone wrote for an hour, and when it was time for the students to read their work aloud, one young girl rose and spoke of her father molesting her—that very morning it had happened, and it had been going on for years.

Suddenly it became an emergency. The librarian called the teachers, the teachers called the principal, the principal called the counselor, and the counselor called an off-grounds psychologist. While all this was happening, the kids were hugging the poor abused girl and sharing not only in her happiness that she had finally freed herself of the debilitating silence but also in the sorrow of her suffering.

Her poem meant a fresh start, a way to begin the recovery process. (The first order of the day was to arrest her father, which the police did.) It was a profound moment in that classroom and one of the most meaningful and consequential uses of poetry I've ever witnessed. Of course, it is not something that happens in my classroom—or any classroom—every day. Nonetheless, one must find a way to teach literature so students can begin to engage their freedom of self-expression, to write poetry that alerts them to their importance in the world.

5.

It is important to make poetry real for kids, available to all their senses. Here's what happens: I give each kid in my class an ear of corn (use anything you wish in yours; this is just an example), and I tell them to close their eyes and imagine everything they wanted out of their lives that had never materialized. Each corn leaf represents a memory. "Aggressively tear a leaf from the husk," I instruct them.

Once the corn (their souls or hearts) is stripped bare of bad memories, I ask them to feel and smell the kernels. I tell them to keep their eyes closed and imagine every kernel as a good memory, to find images and sounds and rhymes and rhythms and phrases and nouns and verbs that they think stand for and make up the elements of life—with the sun doing its part, the earth and water theirs. When the kids open their eyes, I ask them to begin writing their vocabulary for joy, for sadness—to begin to work with language to express their emotions in images, assonances, alliterations, metaphors. This is just the beginning, of course, a starting point—but hopefully also a turning point in their learning to find poetic tools for expressing their voices.

6.

When a kid is caught in his or her version of no-man's land, with nothing to lose, it is usually interpreted as the kid committed some terrible crime, as the kid did something stupid to sabotage his or her chance for a normal life.

Poetry has the magic to transform that crazy energy for the person's benefit. Poetry can make use of desperation and hopelessness—and once that wild, passionate energy is harnessed, directed, and engaged with focus and purpose, real personal change is possible. No one can anticipate the magnitude of gifts the person will contribute to society's welfare. When poetry engages despair, it's a game changer. Try it in your classroom with the so-called gangbangers, bored kids, troubled, wounded lads—it works wonders.

Feeding the Roots of Self-Expression and Freedom

How should one use this book? The answer is any way that works for you! Read for pleasure, self-reflection, or sharing with others in any setting, or use this as a mentor text in education to teach skills and concepts of life and writing. Throughout the text, research is a component that can be added to enhance understanding and/or to make the topic relevant to the reader. This can be cursory or in-depth to build schema and to promote writing. Reading and writing are forms of thinking. The intent is to share one man's journey, to help the reader think about his or her own journey by reading and writing, and to reflect and act. That is the ultimate that any author can request of the reader. Jimmy Santiago Baca (JSB) shares his personal expectation, once in a darkened corner with himself, through a life-line of letters with one who became a friend, and now with us, a journey that remains in progress, that we can all learn from:

> *"I parade down no street with flute and bandage; I sign no paper of exulting principles. I do what other men and women do, rise in the morning and demand from myself a little more than yesterday."*
> *–Letter excerpt written by JSB to Tucson Poet, Will Inman (WI)*

The lost voices (having only recently been unearthed), yet more accurately, the found voice of Jimmy Santiago Baca and his early prison days are representative of the journey through which JSB traveled not solely by choice, but also by circumstance, to another world and back again. These never before published poems are raw, real, and riveting. His words do not seek your pity or condolences, his words seek readers to nourish their thoughts and move them to be better individuals. JSB writes to Inman,

> *"My poetry has warmed so cold distant worlds and suffering deep in me, as only the light of poetry can with its hope and freedom encircling the world these days. I've endangered the*

existence of all prisons with my blood and tears and fed the roots of self-expression and freedom."
—Letter excerpt from JSB to WI

This self-expression and freedom belongs to you, the reader, for the taking. We, the writers, encourage you to read, think, write, and/or act.

JSB's journey is presented in sections, but need not be read in linear fashion, nor is the suggested curricular guide more than choice. When these poems were written by JSB, there was no intent for "sections," nor does the order reflect his choices. However, Sheehan and VanBriggle determined that it would be a way in which all readers, especially educators or facilitators of writing workshops, might engage readers and provide a broad context. It is simply a collection of ideas and questions that may help educators to plan instruction and take readers beyond the authors' collective thoughts as they are presented.

The first glimpse into JSB's journey begins with nightmarish undertones in the real world. It is a world that demands and supports **Dehumanization Process**. As JSB is assimilated into the prison world he began **Journeying Inward**. This became a time of deep self-reflection and JSB's voice is full of extremes in experience and emotion. Throughout the rollercoaster of actions and reactions, Jimmy Santiago Baca begins **Illuminating Outward** and he begins to develop an appreciation of the good that exists in life and learns how to capture its essence. His voice sings. Although moments of bleak and dark voice still exist, there is a change in the writing. The final series of poems exist within a section entitled **Rehumanization Process**. Although physically still confined, Jimmy Santiago Baca's voice begins to soar and flickers of freedom abound.

Dehumanization Process

32
The Price Is Never Too High

A politician cannot curb the crime rate
because his methods attack the wrong problems,
but when the public clamors he is very
business-like and offers them samples
of what the real thing is like,
A man in chains, and they wait and wait
for the crime rate to drop but it never does.

Maybe the politicians are asking the wrong questions; therefore, the wrong solutions are provided. This sentiment not only begins the discussion about correctional facilities and legislation, but also opens the door to other dialogue that is relevant to our lives today.

- **What questions should be asked?**
- **Who should be asking and of whom?**
- **Is justice just?**

Reading and writing about comparative responses builds the schema or background one has and lends itself to critical thinking, debate, and argumentative essays. The reader may wish to investigate the controversial ideology that the impetus for building prisons is often based upon the second or third grade literacy scores in a given state. This is often referred to as an urban myth, yet many news stories and articles have been written to the contrary.

- **What are the crime statistics in your area? (both adult and juvenile)**
- **Are the statistics considered valid, real; how do you know?**
- **What can society do to lessen the crime rate?**
- **Is there or could there be legislative actions that could help in some way?**

- **Is there a way you can become involved?**

These are not only questions for individuals with freedoms. If one is or has been incarcerated, consider the following:

- **Where and when did you begin to encounter problems? (connect to one's own circumstances)**
- **What could have helped you then?**
- **What can help you now?**
- **How can you help yourself?**

What thoughts does one have about any of these issues? How does this affect you? Does it affect you? **Tell your story** in conjunction with what you find through research.

> Ultimately, one may ask, "What Does It Matter? We have our students read great works of literature to give them opportunity to think deeply about the issues that will affect their lives. After students are able to answer the two questions "What does it say? and "What does it mean?" (Gallagher, 2004, p. 89).

Gallagher (2004) continues to state that readers are provided practice, a life-rehearsal without consequence, and a way to explore the issues and find the relevance of the themes in literature as a whole. Story is the way in which we communicate our histories. Jimmy Santiago Baca shares his journey of enlightenment with all who choose to read it for just that reason, to provide a context for the reader to share in his story, but also to create one's own.

62
They Are Humans

**It took humans to build this prison-
how many, 500? 1000?**

They *are* humans, but the questions remains:
- **Is there humanity?**
- **Does humanity exist within the prison system?**

These probing questions have the possibility to open doors that one may not have thought about without prompting. Another parallel

that can be introduced here is to discuss:
- **Who resides in the prisons?**
- **Is it choice or circumstance?**

Possible Paired Reading:
"The Cold Within" (Poem) James Patrick Kenny (n.d.)

Another lesson to consider may be the use of numbers in literature/poetry. The symbolism of numbers and meanings can be seen as far back as history exists.

- **What connections can be made to numbers and writing? What connection can be made within your life?**
- **Re-read "They Are Humans." Why were those numbers utilized?**
- **Was this usage planned or arbitrary? Although readers may never know the answer, does it really matter? Think of what they symbolize.**
- **What do numbers in a prison, a school, a university, at work represent?**
- **What *do* those numbers represent to you the reader?**
- **How do these numbers speak to you?**
- **Write utilizing the symbolism of numbers about a subject you have passion for and that can move the reader to discussion or action.**

Cross-Curricular Connections:
- If some connections are needed to explore this further, think in terms of all content areas. Mathematics is an obvious beginning.
- The numerology of the past in many ancient civilizations that lends itself to today's math is a good beginning. One might also consider Pythagorean ideology.
- Religious connections that are seen not only in religious documents, but also in world literature.
- The use of numbers is far reaching and has significance in all societies and includes different cultural understandings.
- The numerology of myth and let's not forget art portrayed as realistic or myth. For example, the artwork of *Ruben's Judgment of Paris (Ruebens, c. 1625)* which depicts the story of Paris and the apple to the fairest woman, and the trio is shown in this intricate *artwork*. To engage students use symbolism from

contemporary society and the language of gangs may surface in this discussion.

- What numbers are a part of your life? How can those numbers be connected to writing? To others?

Another connection would be to read about historical parallels such as the use of conscripted individuals and/or slaves to build The Great Wall or the Pyramids.

Prior to reading the trilogy of poems entitled "***Depersonalization Step 1***," "***Depersonalization Step 2***," and "***Depersonalization Step 3***" participate in a three-to-five-minute free-write:

- **What does it mean to depersonalize or dehumanize another human being? Is it done today? In our society? Respond in any way that works for you as a writer.**
- **Turn and talk with an individual near you.**
- **List group ideas and discuss.**
- **If you read simply for pleasure, think about these ideas and make a personal connection.**

If this book is being used for instruction, provide some background for individuals who may need more information prior to reading or have students research and provide the background for the group. For example, as far back as ancient Egypt and Rome, societies have been using the process of dehumanization to control individuals and groups without little thought for what this means to the society as a whole.

This practice of treating others as subhuman has continued through the ages of slavery in our nation. The Holocaust was an exercise in genocide that was known world-wide and genocide continues even in today's world. Names of places such as Darfur, Burundi, and Rwanda are known world-wide for such evils.

- **Is the process of dehumanization about control? Why or why not? What evidence exists?**
- **How does it create an opportunity to view another as "subhuman"; therefore, rendering those individuals as a non-entity and worthless?**
- **Does removing moral responsibility make it easier to inflict pain, be it mental or physical? Explain your answer.**
- **Is dehumanization a deliberate action?**

Whether deliberate or not, dehumanization does exist in our world today. It existed in Jimmy Santiago Baca's world when he was incarcerated.

If you are an individual reading poetry for personal pleasure or enrichment, you know what to do—skip over the classroom instructions and just read or use the questions as a guide for your thinking.

If you are in a classroom or reading and/or responding with a facilitated group, read each of the poems that follow closely. As you read the passages, mark and annotate or code the text. Highlight words you do not know, find interesting, or that need more explanation to clarify the context. Paraphrase for meaning and examine the speaker, his tone and narrative voice. Write any questions you have in the margins.

- **Turn and talk in small groups to share your thoughts and ideas.**
- **Read each selection aloud to the class. A fluent model can provide clarity of understanding for some individuals. Ask students to continue to mark the text, but in a different color for each reading.**
- **Ask students to return to their small groups and discuss any new ideas, questions, etc.**
- **What are the ways that dehumanization is portrayed in these three poems?**
- **You may ask students to determine how the poems narrate Jimmy's history and/or present facts versus observations.**
- **At this point a free-flow of ideas and questions should propel the discussion and writing.**

Cross-Curricular Connections:
- View dehumanization in historical context using the above method and connecting it to JSB's poems.
- Research genocide and how it begins and develops.
- A mathematical approach may be to look at and collect statistics of genocide and/or prison states and present factual numbers within this context.

Possible Paired Readings:
Holocaust Fiction and/or non-fiction, or young adult literature related to the Holocaust

Letters From Rifka (2009) Karen Hesse

Genocide in Elie Wiesel's *Night: Social Issues in Literature* (2004) Louise Hawker

Genocide in Anne Frank's, *The Diary of a Young Girl: Social Issues in Literature* (2001) Louise Hawker

Read the next three poems and reflect upon JSB's words and connect your thoughts. Annotating the text will be helpful, even to the reader who reads for pleasure.

75
Depersonalization: Step 1

The new recruits are jammed in seats
with barred windows and chains
undulating everywhere. The bus parks
outside the walls in blazing sunlight.
A sooty smoke stack and clean steeple
poke up from the walls: "That's
the death house and that's the church,"
offers an old timer back again, he says,
because he gets lonely out in society
and wants to see his friends again.
The young eyes fixed on the steeple
and then the smoke stack; some feign
bravery and laugh about it all,
monomaniacs cackling about their adventures
with the law and ladies. A sharp silence
pierces their hearts when the big gates open.
There is a quivering fear in their veins,
a helpless wailing in the quiet of their eyes,
"Let me out! I don't belong here...I am
confused, lonely, sick, jobless, homeless,
I need help, I don't belong here!"
But nobody listens or even will ask about
how you feel, you are a convict now,
not a human being, a convict, got it?
You don't feel, you don't love, you are
not to show kindness, you are a beast
of burden, and you are here to work
and wait, work and wait, work and wait.

76
Depersonalization: Step 2

The nights grow lonelier, lonelier,
and you are a new-born fetus in this womb of hell,
the pain and the hurt of growth come like never
before.
You must cuss to be cool, walk like a young bull,
rip-off the commissary of younger inmates, carry a
shank,
take drugs…you must grow into these things…
confusion wrenches your heart into dark tangles,
you are caught in a suffocating web, helpless,
suspended like a chunk of meat before butchers,
your soul has caught on the heavy hook of despair,
slowly molding, blistering into raw sores,
and each day comes with another handful of salts
your hopes and dreams become heavy blocks of rock
on your shoulders, as they gradually slump
and the sweet limbs of the spirit are amputated
and trampled by so much darkness,
and you toss the dead matter of hopes and dreams
away like something illegal and evil;
your tools are racism and violence, deception
and a knife…a child of prison now.

77
Depersonalization: Step 3

New recruits come into the cell block,

there are hoots and whistles. Someone
was murdered this morning and you stop to talk
and joke half-heartedly with others. They make way
as the stretcher is wheeled in and the dream man
taken away. The crumbled receipt of goods;
a ragged bag of sunburned wrinkles, tobacco stained
fingers and gums, the same old denims and number,
a tan brogan dangling out of the sheet,
brown apologetic eyes, graying hair, and crinkled
lips,
all tossed into the wastebasket of a prison graveyard,
like an insignificant book of dreams
on the shelf since anyone can remember, collecting
dust,
no one ever cared to read it, a society too busy,
a prison too blind, its pages yellowed, it was a
thousand
years old some say, and it has become dust again.
The barber goes back to snipping hair,
the porters go back to slopping the tiers,
you go to your cell, adjust the TV,
make some hot coffee and watch "All in the Family."

As you read the following quote, think of what it means to you and how it connects to the three preceding poems:

- *"People will rarely remember what you did, but they will always remember how you made them feel" (Author unknown).*

  What does this quote mean to you? How does this relate to the readings and discussions about dehumanization? Write, turn and talk to share. Help each other to make connections.

- List ways that the process of dehumanization is used in today's society.

  Reminders if the group is unable to come up with ideas: Bullying, home situations (domestic violence/child abuse), our prisons, etc. This is a great place for making text-to-text connections of young adult and/or classical literature, text-to-self (one's own world), and text-to-world (that world can be home, school, play, or global).

- Can we change the idea and implementation of dehumanization? Do we wish to change it?

- Write a poem: *Dehumanization is…*or respond to the discussions of the past days.
- Engage in other extension activities and/or cross curricular connections.
- Place an individual or personified individual (the prisons, the schools, and the workplace) on trial for participation in the dehumanization process.
- Have you ever been the victim or aggressor in such an action? If so, how did it make you feel?
- As an extension activity ask students to write a letter of apology to one's victim if he or she was the aggressor, or a letter to the aggressor if he or she was victimized.
- Discuss and/or research local prisons and/or juvenile facilities. Pose the question: Can/Should a prison run without implementing this dehumanization process? Why or why not? Great topic for research and oral debate.
- Is there a process that would provide the "control" that could replace this process?
- Create a public service announcement (PSA) in video form or as a podcast—the message is up to you.
- Perform a dramatic interpretation (music/dance/acting) of any of the three poems written by JSB or an interpretation of your understanding.
- Create a work of art that represents one or all of the poems.

Possible Paired Readings:

Night (1960) Elie Wiesel
Without Sanctuary: Lynching Photography in America (2000) James Allen
Readings on Apartheid
Readings on the Lucifer Effect (dehumanization) by Philip Zimardo (Stanford University)

Again, if you read these poems simply for the pleasure of reading, don't get caught up in the curricular suggestions. These are merely "talking points" for extended discussions. You may wish to consider a book club to look closely at some of the topics that are brought to the surface and consider action, or use it solely for discussion.

63-64
Waking Up in Prison

With a violent tear, the vengeful disembodied voice,
screeches over the loud speaker:
sudden, like a stake driven into my brow,
the bones of my skull splintered,
as it rips through the silky mist of my dreams,
crushing the images of ones I long for,
of places I've come from and been to.

Crushing my grandfather's rocking chair,
the black old pot-bellied stove,
darkening the sad red flames dancing on mud walls,
disfiguring the ancient bronze face,
the lips withered like rose leaves,
the silver hair bunned up,
torn apart, the image buckles under,
like a struggling doe shot in the heart,
its knees crumple, and its great brown eyes
look at you, dismayed, astonished, hurt.

As the voice comes to crushing, hurtles down,
an upheaval of boulders breaking and jolting down,
with scissor-like edges, down upon my heart,
violently suffocating it...

The racks of cell doors crack open agonized
like old coffins whose nails scratch,
unwilling to open, petrified graves,
unwilling to release the living, breathing dead.

Four cells away a friend of mine walks out,
sleepy eyed, he greets me, "Want a cigarette?"
as if he knew what I had been through, "Ya" I say.
With our hands punched into our coat pockets,
we walk down the tier, down the stairwell,
across the main floor of the cellblock,
and outside to the landing,
where there is a real sky and still a few stars,
where we inhale fresh air, cold and clean,
and our breath gleams out in balloons against
the compound's brilliant spotlights.

We walk across the twilight compound to the kitchen,
Beneath my tongue I taste the emptiness of another day,
like a capsule of poison, and with my first cup of coffee,
it slowly pops, dissolves under my tongue,
slowly numbing my heart,
still moist from last night's dream of back home.

Engagement in any writing workshop requires attention to words. The words of Jimmy Santiago Baca create images that one cannot ignore and evoke emotion that one must release.

- In the preceding poem, "Waking Up in Prison," identify the images of life and death, both real and metaphorical.
- Does the way that one perceives death have consequence as to how life is lived?
- Identify the imagery and the extremes within this poem that speak loudly to you, the reader. What does it say to you? For example, the reality of waking up in prison is in opposition to the longing for life beyond bars and waking from the dream is like waking to die each day. The imagery of death in the "struggling doe" in the text awakens the reader to the harshness and immediate reality of this life.
- Appoint group facilitators and engage in discussion about the poem and ask students to conclude where and how the metaphor is carried and to highlight and annotate the text. Have students investigate different metaphors for death and write some poems.

- If an individual chooses, writing about the opposite, birth in metaphorical terms, could also provide a perspective to the discussions and allow for comparing and contrasting.
- This mentor text, "Waking Up in Prison," shows how a metaphor is carried throughout a piece of writing. What other intangible items can be made tangible by metaphor? Using a metaphor, create a poem that speaks about an aspect of one's own life.

Possible Paired Readings:
Investigate metaphors of death in works such as *Hamlet, Frankenstein,* or the *Odyssey*.

> In the splintered sections of letters, Inman writes to Baca,
> *"I really loved your letter—you sound like a strong-spirited guy. 'I write poetry as a rock-breaker breaks rocks.' Man! There's a poem in itself… It is very clear to me that you have a style of your own, a range of vision and approaches, and a strong use of the language."*
>
> *Letter excerpt from WI to JSB*

Much like the fragmented pieces of JSB's life, letter fragments between Baca and Tucson poet Will Inman exist and are shared throughout this text. Inman symbolically threw a life-line to JSB during his prison years and helped him to find his voice through questioning, acknowledgments, facilitation, and friendship all through the power of the written word in letters. As educators, or facilitators of writing workshops, the opportunity exists to use Jimmy's words and one's knowledge of the community within which one works.

> *"Life is a splendorous kaleidoscope, but in our rapid fall, we see only the blur; the rope burns on our souls as we try to grip and lose our courage, pain of the body slams our hearts aside, upends our well-ordered morals like a table of golden trophies, and we sit in the destruction; despair drives some to attach others; damage submits others to fold-up, and within the folds lets Willpower mold green, a slip spot, moist for eggs of Tyranny."*
>
> *Letter excerpt from JSB to WI*

- What is contained in your "kaleidoscope of life"?

- **What controls your actions?**
- **Does it affect the actions of others?**
- **Begin to look within at one's own "range of vision and use of strong language" that defines you as an individual.**

5

My Inability to "Adhere"

Those in the way of history
Will be labeled as "unable to adhere"
Discarded like the Indians
who could not "adhere".
I am looked upon for twenty-four hours a day,
no sunshine, no entertainment,
ill health due to cramped conditions,
and immense frustration.
It's not illuminating
as one riding into a conquered town
on a white stallion;
more like Paul Revere galloping
to tell everyone the tyrants are coming
and finding empty eyes and vacant sleepy heads,
quite submissive and willing to be drawn
under kind-hearted yokes.
So here I am, pondering the clash of violence,
oppression, the killing of souls,
the stale smell in the air
that jolts the heart like big rifles,
as the bullets of violence and frustration,
kill the souls; kill creativity, God's creation,
those white doves, root up red roses,
leaving empty eyes, rootless lives of men.

Re-read the fragment of a letter from above and "My Inability to Adhere." Some ideas to consider while reading: Are roots, physical or mental, what secure us and make us strong? Write about your roots—are they strong, weak, or entangled?

- **Do we all have roots? Think about how far your roots go?**
- **What can break the roots? How does this affect your life?**
- **What is your personal inability to adhere? Write about it.**
- **How do the two readings go together? Do they? Write to explain, analyze, or simply provide reflection.**
- **Using the fragment as a model text, provide a stem for writers, "Life is..." and invite them to use vivid language.**

Cross-Curricular Connections:
- Use artistic expression (any medium) to represent your roots.
- What other groups in society have been considered "unable to adhere"?

74
Letters Come to Prison

White doves
crashing through the layers
of ice in the air,
and land warmly
in freezing palms of cons.

- **What symbolism can be found and how does that connect the reader to the words?**
- **What importance are letters to those who are incarcerated?**
- **Can letters be a detriment?**
- **Have letters ever played an important role in your personal life?**
- **Many individuals today correspond only using technology. What if that technology to connect you to friends, family, and the world were unavailable. How would you and/or your life change?**
- **How will history record great correspondence between individuals in the years to come?**
- **Is it possible we can lose our history, our culture and more because of today's innovation and new technologies? Will it matter?**
- **Think of a time when you made a "wrong" choice in life. Write**

a letter to yourself dated a few days before the incident.

Extension Activities and Cross-Curricular Connections:
Letter writing is becoming a lost art form in our society. Just as storytelling waned after writing became the trend, letter writing in today's world of instant gratification is waning as well.

- Discuss the uses for writing letters throughout history and famous correspondents over the ages and how this affects cultures. It may include dignitaries, lovers, academia, business, etc.
- Create letters (including all the artistic nuances) from past eras.
- Create a letter to your best friend about your "inability (or ability) to adhere."

Possible Paired Readings:
Letters of Abelard and Heloise, *The Love Letter of Abelard and Heloise* (1901) Gollarez & Horten—Translation
Letters of John and Abigail Adams (@1782)
Letters/Writings of Benjamin Franklin or Thomas Paine

6
A Life of Chance

Each day appears a coin-stacked table,
white chips of my life,
lined up like old buffalo's teeth,
in wavering heat of their hunger
were drawn to silvery desert pools, unaware.

Soft fingertips of Hope
on cool rims of my skull
slide along,
tips for openers gamble my life
on a bluff hand,

For tomorrow rides in from the horizon,
a bloodless gunslinger
with cards up his sleeve,
sitting across from us
we never know
when he raises his head,

if it's to draw his gun
or buy us a beer.

1

It's Not What I Want but What Must Be

Our happiness is a thing of the past,
we did what we thought was best,
in this world with violence,
religious fanatics and love so false.
With time, the keepsakes we keep melt,
the impressions of sadness on our feelings melt,
the memoirs go away, they also melt,
even though I don't understand or wish to believe it,
that we who made all of it, could destroy all of it,
perhaps, our riches of love were too much for the
heart,
a heart that shows its face to the world, is destroyed,
this much we know, and somehow go on living.

After reading "A Life of Chance*" and "It's Not What I Want But What Must Be," consider the following:

- **Think about the difference between choice and chance? Are they the same?**
- **What if we never took a chance?**
- **Write to present your views: Chance, choice, fate…Do we let things happen to us, encourage them, or deter them?**
- **Other areas to examine in terms of the surrounding world and how one fits in it, is examining how do we survive the un-survivable in history, in current events, and in our own lives? What are those events and how are you personally affected?**
- **Think about the idea of keepsakes, those things we hold important. What does it mean "…*the keepsakes we keep melt*"? Is this something we, society—individuals, do to ourselves or is it put upon us?**

In the poem that follows, "Little Difference," consider the question, "How does one move from childhood to *here*?" Depending on where "here" currently is, a different answer will exist.

- Ask readers to think about their own childhood and consider where they are now as the poem is read aloud. Individual readers can also read the poem aloud to experience that sensory effect. Individuals can brainstorm about who am I, where do I come from, and more. Turn this into a full piece of writing.
- Dissect how to change "fate" through a course of action or lack of action. Looking at one's own life, what would make a difference or what could have made a difference?
- Is society doomed to repeat its mistakes, collectively and/or individually?

Cross-Curricular Connections:
- This is also a terrific connection to historical and current events and social justice where research and writing in all forms can provide not only great conversation about the world around us, but also to comprehend how one fits within it.
- The idea of social justice permeates much of today's young adult literature, contemporary fiction, and non-fiction. This idea is also found in graphic novels, varied medias, artwork, lyrics, poetry, and the news. Seek out connections that speak to you.

43
Little Difference

I listen to the same songs on the radio,
Here in this little cubicle of 5x9,
Playing Rummy with my celly,
Who asks who is that singing?
Bet it's Lou Rawls. I said, Nope.
He won the bet and lightly punched
Me in the arm.
Except for the few gray hairs on my head,
These days piled up like worn out shoes,
Not much has changed in the last ten years,
I'm still listening to the same old songs,
In prison again, playing Rummy with my celly.

Read the poem "Life" aloud and think about, but do not share aloud the following:

- **What is your reaction? Do you react?**
- **What is the speaker telling us?**

Individuals may choose to free-write answers or simply "hold" the answers inside.

40
Life

Here on my bed,
I watch a spider crawl down the wall,
Mmm (he pauses),
then carefully toes forward,
with the a pinched foothold,
kinky legs cringe,
through pesticide fume-mines.

I close my eyes for a moment,
then open them to see him
belly dive on my bed,
and begin to spin a silk tent
in the brown army wool.

Friends,
we respect each other,
until tonight,
brave hunter
with weapons of silk
and patience.
Today—my comrade,
Tonight my enemy.

- **Now re-read the poems silently and mark the text and determine what else one can discern from a deeper reading. Turn and talk in small groups to share ideas for readings 40 and 43.**

- Identify themes or ideas that require some discussion. If the reader is not making connections, here are a few ideas that may get the conversation moving:
- Look at the phrase ..."*through pesticide fume-mines.*" Determine what this might refer to in a setting of incarceration. How does the speaker's world compare to that of the spider? To that of your world?
- The idea of a poison life abounds throughout many of the poems. Are there connections students can make to other poems?
- Another theme herein is the concept of friendship. In the world where the spider and JSB exist, there are pseudo friendships. Do pseudo friendships exist in our own lives? If so, why do they exist? How does this differ from "real" friendship?
- Think about a place and time where one must always be on guard, spinning a web of one's own to stay safe, attack, or deal with the circumstance of life is at that moment. Write about a time when being on guard or "spinning a web" was necessary.

This is also a great opportunity to discuss metaphors such as spinning a web and how such a technique can add to one's ability to "say it" without "directly" stating a thought, willing the reader to think and connect.

Possible Paired Readings:
Looking at foils in literature (individuals who contrast one another and/or whose differences illuminate important characteristics in the other) one may wish to read about the following:

Mercutio and Tybalt in *Romeo and Juliet*
Bertha and Jane Eyre in *Jane Eyre*
Jekyll and Hyde in *Dr. Jekyll and Mr. Hyde*

Journeying Inward

If you are reading this in a linear fashion, there is a parallel to the ideology of a "hero's journey." It is obvious that the first section symbolizes the point at which everything changes for JSB, our hero exemplar. The first three steps (Poems numbered 75-77—JSB's numbering of the poems which was kept intact) provide the harsh realities or consequences to his actions. He finds himself alone, unknowing and in need of "something," but just what he cannot grasp. His anger surfaces in the text, but he has yet to develop a source of this anger. There are many who choose the hero's journey, yet equally as many who do not choose it, yet find themselves thrust into it unknowingly.

JSB's journey was not only a physical acclimatization, but a spiritual one as well. He has no supernatural aid as in many of the journey stories, but he does have Tucson poet Will Inman, who becomes not only a teacher and friend, but also a spiritual guide of sorts enticing JSB to answer his own questions. The poems that follow show some of the trials and tribulations JSB faced as he begins the horrific journey inward, into the bowels of the prison and that of his soul.

> *"How I have grown has been to laugh with the broken ones,*
> *How I have lived is to learn to sleep on a bed of snakes coiled*
> *like steel springs at my back. I live between two wrongs as a*
> *right unto myself and I growl at my trespassers."*   ***JSB to WI***

> **2**
> **I Stand Confused**
>
> **In fear of the games the world plays,**
> **All-important to the way of God they say,**
> **Games that bring greater shame and violence.**
> **Kiss the blue rim of guns,**
> **For if they are to be lonely**
> **They must enjoy their loneliness.**
> **The CIA will sell your heroin,**
> **The government their black chains,**
> **Huddled in dungeons we decay in our own**
> **   rejection.**

- **Please note that throughout the text (as above) the format of the poetry is Baca's in its raw form. It is presented as written and is part of the poet's message.**

- Have a discussion about this poem, "I Stand Confused," that confronts your own sense of confusion about something in your life and connect it to what Baca states. How are the realities similar? Different?
- Is life a game and if so, is there a winner? Create pros and cons for a negative and positive response to this question. Provide evidence from this text and others that may support your point of view.
- Reflect upon the phrasing "...*we decay in our own rejection.*" Engage in a three-minute free write that explains what this means to you. Take this piece of writing and extend it to add substance to your writing.
- Look at the brevity of this poem and discuss what makes word choice in poetry and/or other genres important.
- Discuss some of life's mixed messages and confusion—look at your personal circumstances as well.
- How do the poem and the letter excerpt pair, or do they? Remember to use examples from the text to present your point of view.
- Write your own poem about confusion.

Cross-Curricular Connection:

- Now, in small groups, share your answers. Discuss current events in the past 10 years that connect to the phrase, **"...*we decay in our own rejection,*"** and the American way of life. Research your choices and provide evidence and quotes from those texts and be sure to cite them accordingly. (Examples: Enron, current events rallying against systems, etc.)

Possible Paired Reading:
The Jungle (1906) Upton Sinclair—(Systematic reforms, labor history, immigration, brutality)

55

This Hatred

Forming in this prison emptiness,
drop by drop down from cell ceilings,
onto the open staring eye,

Until it turns it cold,
gleaming hard as any blade,
red and cold and empty,

Till the look once soft and human
scratches at your glassy heart,
society.

"When you, for example, an individual with every valid excuse
to surrender, to let his spirit fall apart, to become bitter and
degenerate, when you decide to build and nurture meaning
in your life by the way you relate to others and by creating in
your poems that is a direct manifestation of the Holy Spirit,
no matter what particular religion that Spirit may take name
from, and is to be revered and loved. At the same time, it is
you, personally, individually, and that, too is to be revered and
loved. Not flattered. Not ass-kissed. But shared with, sung with,
laughed with, wept with, been human with. So that's where
I am in my reach to you. I feel that is where you are in your
reach to me, too. And it is good!"   ***WI to JSB***

- Compare and contrast the two writings. Provide evidence from the text to promote your analysis.
- What propels people to "hate"? Define "hate" using a modified concept ladder.
- Can hate ever be a mechanism for survival? Provide examples for discussion and use textual evidence to present an argumentative essay.
- How does hatred develop?
- How does one examine self-hatred? How does one begin to identify it?
- Thinking about the concept of "hate or hatred," write a *call to action* for individuals to participate in an action against hate. Use the idea of social justice and cases that have been in the news now and in the past. How can one person or a small group of individuals make a difference?
- Look at the language used to describe society in "This Hatred." If the wording were changed (you decide how), how would the poem's meaning change?

Cross-Curricular Connection:
- What does hatred look like? Create a piece of artwork, 2D or 3D, that represents hatred. Write a poem that echoes this visual piece.
- Present performance poetry that captures the essence of what hatred "looks like."

Possible Paired Readings:
"The Cold Within" James Patrick Kinney (n.d.)
October Mourning: A Song for Matthew Shepard, Leslea Newman (2012)

15
The Guards, Judge & Society

Your harsh words
cannot pound the door down,
I open to you with kind words,
you cannot make barren
the branches I extend to you,
the buds open at my breath,
the hostility in your eyes
cannot shrivel my love to a bruise,
when my wounds are healed I will toss you the scabs,
give you the end of my suffering your pretty leaf
tongues can lick,
not the beginning when I need you most,
give you the smile I never gave myself,
the hand that was never there for me,
when you fall, I will be the silence
when you escape with your secrets,
the words you want to say and cannot,
the love when you hate yourself.
I will do these things for you.
I will be the cups at your lips when you awake,
the cold water you splash over your face,
your work trousers, your stockings,
I will smoke cigarettes and talk with you,
late into the night, and sleep late with you,
you are one of those people, who is not perfect,
and I am one of those people who do not want you to be.

Re-read the following lines from the "The Guards, Judge &
Society": **"give you the smile I never gave myself/the hand that was
never there for me"** This brings to mind the maxim, "treat others the
way you wish to be treated, not how you are treated."

- What other maxims can be identified in relationship to this poem?
- Why is this considered a maxim and not an aphorism or adage? Is it a true maxim? Compare and contrast the differing types of proverbs, maxims, adages, aphorisms, etc. and write to decide if they should or should not be utilized in writing.
- What is JSB telling the guards, the judges, and society? Use evidence from the text to affirm your position.

Cross-Curricular Connection:
- Write a poem from a different era of history to the guards, judges, and/or society. (Example: During prohibition, World War I or World War II, the Harlem Renaissance, etc.)

27
Shake Down

Into my cell
The guards come in as I am
Sitting down here on my bed,
Enjoying myself for no reason,
Distracted by loud noises,
Failing to keep my schedule,
I am happy though, like grass,
Able to accept lovers
Or brush fires, curious inspectors
As the guards check my asshole,
My foot soles, behind my ears
And ask me to shake my hair out,
As if milkweeds and they were looking
For a four-leaf clover or lost penny
In the tall wild grass I am today.

- Compare and contrast the images used in the poem to the harsh realities of the actions. Draw some conclusions as to why these pairings work in the poem? Or take the opposition if you believe they do not.
- In what ways is your day filled with shakedowns? Write to explain in prose or poetry.

- **What enduring humiliations lessen one's humanity? Use evidence from the poem to begin the conversation and/or writing and make connections to other curricula and/or current events.**
- **Is humiliation a form of control? Provide examples to establish your claim.**

Cross-Curricular Connections:
- Look at the use of humiliation in societies worldwide (current and past). Does this humiliation cross lines with human rights? Explain.
- Focus on a human rights issue and write to inform others and provide open-ended questions to help lead the reader to solutions. After sharing aloud, have a discussion of the issue. Great topic for an oral debate focus.
- In law, journalism, etc., the use of social action questions to promote letters to the editors, investigate law cases, etc., is prevalent. What social action questions can you ask? Now write to inform the public.
- Look at and read closely primary source documents that connect to human rights and/or social actions. Connect them to JSB's poem above.
- In English/Reading classes, pair a piece of fictional text with primary source documents from a court case (obviously the two must have a commonality) and use them to facilitate discussions, write essays, and/or editorial pieces.
- In science and/or social science classes, look at the way humiliation leads to actions and/or consequences. Investigate the psychology behind these phenomena.
- How can your findings move individuals to action?

Possible Paired Readings:
Getting Away with Murder: The True Story of Emmett Till (2003) Chris Crowe
Mississippi Trial, 1955 (2003) Chris Crowe
Other connections to Emmett Till include song lyrics (Dylan), and *Jet* Magazine (Sept. /Oct., 1955).

38
Police (Huda)

Squeeze your leather-plated fingers
around Chicano throats,
send your crazed dragons to char the barrio,
from your mouth bullets rip
the streets with unemployed, hunger lines of people.
Muscle-minded badged brutes,
the sleepy populace in rocking chairs with
Bible and flag,
will not bother you,
terrified to stumble forth and say their peace,
no words or destination,
in security, in prejudice, in fear,
the message of apathy creaks in the wind.

I am tired of you killing,
it's a knotted and spliced,
tangled old heap of film,
asleep in the cobwebs the audience snores.
A few escape your guns, their skulls gashed,
blood pours from their faces,
clubbed and disfigured spirits
grasping, heaving wounded,
push above the muck
of cold bugles and drums of blind marchers.

These few in the sweet struggle
to be human beings again
plow brilliant fields of hope,
they see all that bloom new tongues.

This is a poem that can easily be used to show tone and imagery working together. If we remember that tone is simply the author's attitude toward the audience shown through setting, vocabulary choice, and imagery. Do not confuse it with mood, which is the atmosphere created in the feelings of the reader created by those words.

- **Describe the author's tone. This is best done in small groups at first that can lead to a group discussion. Provide evidence from the text.**
- **What is "…the message of apathy (that) creaks in the wind"?**

- Where do we find apathy in today's society? In your immediate community? In your personal life?
- Look at the last stanza of the poem. What does this signify to the reader?

39
Loneliness

After four months in prison,
he received the letter this morning,
"I can't take it any longer,"
she said, and was leaving him.
He stared past the wire fences,
sunlight dumped into the fields,
the wind looped around
billowing mobs of green leaves
gawked at him until a few tore loose,
sailing in the husky breeze away,
sweeping across the field
until out of sight.
He turned and walked to breakfast,
saw a rose petal sunning on the sidewalk,
and smeared it with the heel of his dirty brogan,
leaving a permanent stain of red,
parallel to the highest grief on earth,
only he and the moon would understand,
how it is when all the curtains are dropped,
and the only person who came to see you has left,
will not let you leave the darkness.

"None of us is Pollyanna, none of us avoids facing the real pain and difficulty, but all of us can see beyond it, work within it, not because we dig pain and difficulty, but because we're like salamanders—we can sit at the edge of the water with half our eyes under the surface and half our eyes in the air, able to see inward and outward at the same time."   WI to JSB

- Coping with pain inflicted upon individuals is handled in many ways. In what ways does the speaker handle his pain, or does he?
- How do you handle the loss of love, life, or pains inflicted upon you?

- Is pain ever self-inflicted?
- In the letter excerpt from WI to JSB, what does it mean to see inward and outward at the same time? How does this relate to JSB's journey?

Cross-Curricular Connections:
- How is physical pain a source of reverence in many cultures? Can you identify those cultures and explain this phenomenon?
- Investigate the psychology of pain and the actions and reactions of the receiver.

Possible Paired Reading:
The Things They Carried (1990) Tim O'Brien

24
Freedom Is Mine

It is mine as much as it's anyone's…
This is what I thought
On the mountain that night,
Breathing in the night and moon and stars,
Turning to them, turning to them,
After a hard day on the run from the FBI
Their hired guns in bars and greasy cafes
Looking for a man who had broken his knuckles
Against a wall, pounding and slugging it,
In a rage of love lost and despair.

Do you think they can plunge wires into my brain?
I had swigged a whole bottle of tequila down,
Trying to drown the pain that was like ice,
A fear so cold in my spine I felt neither the crack
Of their clubs at my shoulders
Nor their handcuffs slicing and numbing my wrists
When escorted through county jail halls to my cell.

- In a small group, consider the following and come to a consensus: **"It is mine as much as it's anyone's…/This is what I thought."**
- Define freedom.

- Is freedom physical, psychological, or both? Explain. Provide examples from the text above and/or other texts if you choose to research.
- Is freedom for the taking? Or the giving?
- Is freedom only perceived?
- Identify lines in the poem that speak to the trapping of drink, drugs, or apathy.

Cross-Curricular Connections:
- Locate and read primary source documents insuring freedom in the United States. What evidence from the document is a guarantor?
- Find primary source documents from other countries that either insure or take away freedoms. What evidence from the documents affirms your argument?
- What happens when freedom is taken away?
- Make connections to current events and how they are portrayed in the media. Is this portrayal positive or negative? Does it change with age/gender groups? Where is the evidence to support this?

"It's hard trying to live with two hundred men in the same dormitory. It's hard not to look into their eyes and see hate every day."   *JSB to WI*

25
Paranoia

He looked at me
in his web of fear,
with sensors strict and honed,
with raw clarity for any by passer.
Cuddled in his cell
with dead flies in his food plate,
with a thousand eyes,
he looked at me,
with a dangling thread of hope
saving him from the ultimate abyss,
he looked at me.
Should I come close
he would withdraw,

so I smiled gently
to break his fall,
into the steep cliffs of prison.

Once again author's tone and imagery are at odds, yet seemingly work together.

- **What is the author's tone in "Paranoia"?**
- **What do the speaker's actions show?**
- **Who is paranoid?**
- **What do the "ultimate abyss" and the steep cliffs of prison have in common? In contrast?**
- **Write a piece of poetry that uses the extremes of tone and imagery, yet comes together as one.**
- **Saving another individual saves oneself. Write an argument for this statement. Use evidence from the mentor text and examples from other texts that support your claim.**
- **Think about the small or incidental support(s) you receive daily. Write about a time when someone changed the course of your day with a kindness.**

13
Prison in the Desert

I used to pray
For it sometimes.
Pray that I wake up and find all the compound,
All the buildings,
The stilted hutches of gun towers
Softly shimmering in fresh snow.

It finally snowed
After four years of waiting.
Under a thrusting spray of water
I couldn't hear my friends
Calling me to come see.
After I got out of the shower
And heard everyone talking about snow,
I went to the window to look

What little there was melted.

- What emotion is evoked within the reader after reading "Prison in the Desert"?
- Write about wanting something so much, almost reaching attainment, and then missing the opportunity by seconds.
- Have there been missed opportunities in your life? Write about them in any form.
- How does missed opportunity affect one's future decisions, or does it?
- Write about a time when you should have heeded the words, "Be careful what you wish for."

8

I Am Standing in Front of a Brute

Who wants to off my friend, and I am very scared inside,
but I sidle up next to my friend,
clench my fist, and am ready for the fight.
Sometimes I am in the midst of bullies,
who want this or that from me,
my radio or TV even though I have none,
want me to buy them cigarettes,
and I tell them to take their shit elsewhere.
They get all tuffy and want to kill me
so several times I had to defend myself,
knife someone or beat them with my fists.

I have the edge of surprise on them, that's all,
they have all the firepower and soldiers.
I am walking along quietly
and then turn and pound one in the face,
and then on to the next one.

Prison is an island so far away from water or wind,
nothing is cleared away, the vengeance remains,
the blood clots on older blood,
the stench of men dying is always in the air,
things remain, and rot becomes more rot,
there is only one way out,

and that is to live as fully as possible in suffering,
that is to say turn against all that prison has fancied,
and put yourself on the line of truth,
live and burst through the blood blocks of hate
that inhabit our heavy breast.

*"Ah, man, you have the spiritual force of a saint, and I don't
say that to flatter you but simply to say I recognize what's
happening in you."*   *WI to JSB*

Bullying is not an uncommon topic in the 21st century. It is not a "new" form of torment.

- **Write about a time you stood up for someone who was being bullied or a time that you stood by and watched. Is there anything you would do differently today than you did at the time?**
- **How are belief systems identified and nurtured?**
- **Re-read the poem "I Am Standing in Front of a Brute." Is the speaker JSB forced to endure or to become someone else? Use evidence from the text to discuss and/or write your response.**

Cross-Curricular Connections:
- Research other cases of bullying (physical or emotional, in person or online) that have made public news. What similarities or differences exist in the actions within the poem and the public cases? Be sure to cite evidence from the text.
- Explain why you believe these incidents of bullying made public news.
- These incidents can be utilized for open debate by assigning beliefs and/or allowing individuals to speak for themselves.
- Locate other literature and/or lyrics, etc. that speak out about the incident(s) you researched. Writings may or may not exist. If not, you can create a song, a poster, or other form of writing that expresses the incident and/or your position.
- Write a letter to someone you bullied or someone who bullied you.

Possible Paired Readings:
No Choirboys (2008) Susan Kuklin
Current Events about bullying

50

I Sat by the Big Gates of Prison

Watching some of the convicts unload bread
and ice cream from two trucks.
How burning fire of clear blue
fills the sky today.
I could see the parking lot
filled with trucks and cars.
Fresh air, my friend,
that is what you must be content with,
I told myself.
How easily it is for the ice cream truck,
the bread truck, to come and go each Monday.
Beyond the gate I could see
in the parking lot,
The cars of employees and visitors,
some leaving and others arriving.
Just to think that a little legal paper
can separate me from them so much,
it's unbelievable…a little paper,
does not feel, does not grow, is not human,
and does not know if I am ready for society,
and why does it keep me here, as if so?
If I could cry out to the people,
would they believe me, or the little paper?

- Spend time journaling a list of ordinary objects and events that one sees daily.
- Re-read the list and think deeply about the context these objects and events occur in and list some of the details you may have missed.
- Write creatively about these ordinary objects and/or events.
- What is taken for granted daily? Why is it taken for granted?
- Although society is trying to go "green," the "importance of a piece of paper" affects us all. Identify papers that "define" who we are. Go back to the last line of the poem and connect your list to that line, "…would they believe me, or the little paper?"
- When we look at others, what is it we see?
- When no one is looking at you, how do you behave? Do you behave the same way as if you were being observed? Write a poem about "seeing."

"I am learning to take situations that beat my body to a battered pulp; I am learning to look at myself differently. To see the scattered remnants of hope and dreams, and collect them again: return to my old house after the war, pick through debris for old photos of the mind and soul; glue together my fallen statues of justice and honor, and carefully wrap them in my heart for the long trip back. I am learning."   *JSB to WI*

Possible Paired Reading:
The Importance of a Piece of Paper (2004) Jimmy Santiago Baca

9-12
Around Here

I lose track of time. But I count the days, the days,
by the looks in men's eyes,
by the look of love in my heart, by the number of young men
passing through the big prison gates,
by the mental attrition induced by perpetual tragedy
in peoples' lives,
by the deprivation of freedom and respect I count the days,
and the days and none affect me in the same way,
none are mere numbers
none are holy or holiday, none are feared
they blend and fade into each other as do my ideas with my
heart,
they are massed together,
like the concerted efforts of convicts right now, this moment,
flooding the whole cell block with water and anger,
everywhere,
the screams and destitution of human beings clamor
like the bright midday sun,
is filtered through leaves upon the sleeping heads of citizens,
as the desperate cries and despair,
are filtered in another version on the evening news,
when they say brutal convicts are rioting.

The days get bad;
our conditions get bad, until
something breaks,

the whole prison shakes like a dying man's last breath,
and the days rattle in these steel ribs of bars,
each heart pounding for life,
none wants to die, but already,
already so many this year have,
and the days have befallen,
dressed in the blackest rags of haggard spinsters,
but we have hid the pain our hearts howled to expose,
we have hid the loss in our quiet eyes,
and the heart has made us hate,
has made us more strong, more wild and uncaring,
more willing to give up.

The warden wants to win this battle,
the director of prisons wants to win,
and the days have been mad and shrewd and foul
authoritarians,
brutal and directing our lives,
the days have come upon men and murdered them,
incited them to lose control,
take the chance, lose their lives, take death instead of prison,
instead of cells that slowly suffocate the soul,
instead of more lies from government
the day finds them struck down dead cold and blue in the face.

And people want my poetry to be a social stepping-stone,
not to get their toes dirty with my dead brothers' blood,
not to get it wet in my tears,
they want me to skip along in aristocratic gardens,
they want me to put a chastity belt over my soul,
carry an umbrella like a gentleman,
scribble words about spinster tea parties and spinet pianos,
this they consider fine arts, high poetry.

Forgive me, friends, I cannot comply.
If you raise your hand to your breast in surprise,
gasp in horror at my harsh words, if I snap the delicate stem
of your flowery mind,
and shatter the looking glass of your beautiful world,
it is because of the days,

the days I have seen and tell you about with my heart.

In America, the great writers I know are into prime age,
and unhailed, they struggle
as young men with their works, and are rebuffed
by canine-toothed critics,
because they threaten to invigorate the feeble and gray
literati,
and the critics have not shed a dog's hair
to understand their work,
soupy-eyed critics acquired our great artistic poets,
this is a time of chance and change!
everyone is breaking out of their prison,
and in a time of such change,
their measurement is based upon other value systems,
than the college textbook.
Poetry must be judged by minds willing to arrive at self-
made judgments,
without ridiculous interference, political and religious dogma,
let each decide what the poet's vision is,
let each spurn the confusion the critics hail as enlightenment,
and stop the alienation,
and stop feeling you see one thing and feel one thing,
while you read rubbish and stiff poetry un-tuned to your
experience
you will say, ah! when you read good poetry,
and that is why I write as I do,
because right now two hundred men are sleeping outside,
and six hundred more men are in this building,
are going mad,
flooding the tiers with water, breaking windows out,
burning and screaming and crying,
this is rehabilitation,
these are the days, filled with riots of blacks and whites,
with Chicanos being shot dead,
these are the days, when people tune in on mass murder,
and the TV ratings go up,
when the public is pleased, and tourism increases,
while the blood spilled is the blood of this land,
direct descendants! The very heart of this land,

up in flames! Gone and silenced in their cries of freedom!
Death mediates the condition between people here,
you can have peace if you die here, then you can be free...
Gary Gilmore understood the name of the game,
that prison destroys a man until he is no longer a man.
We have lived the good life so long,
God has always been dependent on to straighten out our lives,
so that when the days bring unexpected disaster,
people will no longer have the strength,
or willpower to carry on,
and their minds distort, become vengeful and pitiful,
we have evolved to a very vulnerable stage,
and we no longer undergo the days of burden with
confidence,
faith has become a black crow of bad luck,
yes, the days, the days, I keep time by people's faces,
I keep time by their hopes and loves,
and I know when there is no love,
then there is no hope,
there is no day,
no time,

I hear the screams of men in the background,
I see the futile lives lost in riots...
I tell people we must be temperate and learn
to restructure our values, and they tell me
go to hell,
put a Saturday night special to my temple,
But what can I tell you?
Look at the date, look at your clock, look at the season,
if it is time to kill,
if it is time to let injustice pass with impunity,
to let people be executed in death chambers,
if your clock says so, if the date says so,
if you have marked the calendar with a red circle...
but I will keep time with my heart, my soul, my eyes and
mind,
by these I count the days.

This one piece of text contains a multitude of subjects to explore.
A close reading to develop deep understanding of this poem will allow the

reader to recognize larger themes and/or expand upon existing themes.

- **Begin by re-reading the text and using text marking and annotation.**
- **Look at the syntax and determine how it adds to or deflects meaning from the words and their meaning.**
- **What is the speaker's attitude toward the audience? Who is the audience?**
- **What does the poem reveal about the speaker?**
- **What images are evoked when reading "Around Here"?**
- **What rhetorical devices (metaphors, similes, symbols, etc.) are employed?**
- **If poets are warriors, then poems are the weaponry. If you were a warrior poet, if you are a warrior poet, what poem would you write?**
- **The notion of counting and time are recurrent themes within this poem. How do you count the days? Write a poem that expresses your notion of counting the days.**
- **Baca personifies the prison, especially in the second section that begins, "The days get bad, …". Re-read this section and discuss how the prison becomes alive with Baca's words and images. Now, write a poem to personify something in your life or personify something from another curricular area that has meaning to your life.**
- **Explain how the speaker changes within the contents of the poem. How does this influence the reader?**

Cross-Curricular Connections:
- Research Gary Gilmore to find out why Baca may have utilized his name.
- Research *Gregg vs. Georgia* and the 8th amendment.
- Research prison riots of historical note and the reasons for the riots, the publicity, and the outcomes. Present the information in small groups and compare and contrast information found about different riots. Are there similarities and/or differences?
- What is prison reform like in your state?
- What are some of the perpetual tragedies experienced in historical context? How might they relate to Baca's experience?

"For days I have watched my enemies load themselves with weapons. I've pondered on possible routes they might take. They stand in groups of five and six, not a hair out of place;

chewing gum, cool-tongued, shoes polished gleaming black.
Why must they start trouble all the time? Why must they attack
my life and my friends? Why must they do what they do? Their
hearts cackle their beaks, their hands move like vulture wings
over everything…"   *JSB to WI*

- How does this quote from the correspondence between the two men fit with the poem "Around Here"?
- If you were to write as Baca to Inman, what quote would be pulled from your correspondence in relation to this poem? What if Inman responded to that communication; what would he state?

26
Riot

Clustered together in rain and guard rifles,
the rain will not wash their skin color away.
With hands behind their heads, nude, in the rain,
black flesh white flesh shimmer,
brown and red flesh glisten.

And see on TV, the blood on white sheets
as they wheel out Billy, a Milker's son,
as they wheel out Otis, a Mechanic's son,
and Gary, nineteen without a person anywhere,

Have you ever thought of them as people?

With these caves you've built in desolate places,
the penitent blood that spills in red seas,
the sacrifice of so many lives on sulfurous rocks,
watching the captive slaves devoured,
gathered around your TV's like a Roman audience…

After reading the letter excerpt from JSB to WI, and the poem "Riot," re-read the following lines from **(9-12) "Around Here ."**
"…these are the days, when people tune in on mass murder,
and the TV ratings go up, when the public is pleased, and tourism
increases…"

- Given the fascination in today's world (21st Century) with reality shows and excessive news programs, how does the media and the public influence violence?
- How is "the system" perpetuated by the public, albeit claims of concern?
- This poem returns the reader to the issue of bullying. Where else in life do we see bullying and/or this type of public display simply for amusement sake?
- The last stanza of this poem creates images that will evoke response in any reader. Using this as a model, create a stanza within a poem that uses this type of imagery.
- The line that remains alone in this poem is "Have you ever thought of them as people?" Where is our humanity? Does it exist? Write to assert your claim on this issue.
- Investigate prison riots in the United States EX: New Mexico Penitentiary Riot (1980), Attica Correctional Facility (Buffalo, NY, 1971), or Oklahoma State Prison (McAlester, 1973).

19-20
Everyday

I meet cold stares of my countrymen,
each eye sharp as an assassin's blade
peeling away my words, cutting into their hearts,
giving me the once over,
then tossing me out of minds as I pass.
Morose and bereaving widowers,
broken with bitterness and loneliness,
a premature aging swells in their youthful being,
wedged into their long dead days,
their dusty silence and concrete tombs.

Holy crosses hang from their necks,
tattoos mark arms and backs
with the blessed Virgin Mary,
faded from toil in the fields
like a harlot's powered cheeks
weeping, smeared with sorrow and drudgery,
sweats cold each night
in the passionate embrace of new wrinkles.

Here in the middle of the desert,
strident wild shrieks are not heard,
no high-pitched howls console these dead,
who have taken faith in life,
like an icon once adored and full of spring's breath,
and hurled it against the bars like atheists,
noble and proud killers and robbers and junkies,
in their own ways; a species of dreamers, romantics,
repelled by stalactical reason,
its defoliated, bare and stale caverns,
they travel through on bloody feet,
over the shiny black rock, refusing to compromise,
their passion and pain,
they become exiles and branded felons.

Ah but no, the land of the dead has something else:
from the dead ones you have pruned their withered
lips,
you have clipped their arms and legs off,
and you build high walls that others may not see,
the inhumanity and degradation of your laboratory,
but listen, and others will listen too,
as the noise grows and grows, creaks
as bones rattle in dark graves,

their souls do not rest,
but spit dust into your rusty eye
Keeper of the dark land, of dark holes of death,
scratched into the earth and filled with human
beings,
whose feelings and ideas and strength of mind,
pierce the tombs with reddened light rays,
not gold or white, but red passion filtering their lives,
their laughter, their love, their pain, their lives.

- The title "Everyday" restores the reader to take notice of the notion of time and its importance. Identify all the ways that time has significance in this poem.
- How is time significant in your life? Write a poem that infers its importance.

- **The idea of death and dying are intertwined in Baca's thoughts here. Do a close reading to identify those images; especially look at the language. Use this as a mentor text to develop your own metaphor.**

Cross-Curricular Connections:
- Many things in life are hidden. Parents hide things from children, children from each other, the government from the public, and prisons in the desert. If we don't see them, are they really there? What is being hidden and why? Discuss entities that fit this category. Choose one to research and/or debate.

Possible Paired Readings:
Information about prisons, mental hospitals, sex trades, the homeless, etc.
Cut (2011) Pat McCormick (mental illness, psychiatric disorders)
Sold (2008) Pat McCormick (sex trade)
One Flew Over the Cuckoo's Nest (1961) Ken Kesey (mental illness)
Speak (1999) Laurie Halse Anderson (date rape, rage, anger)
Impulse (2011) Ellen Hopkins (inside the psychiatric hospital and mental illness)
Slave: My True Story (2005) Mende Nazer (sold into slavery)

16-17
Before Sleep

My soul is caught expanding like a parachute
over the world I live in: Its bony branches,
its winter and roots gag for spring water.
Each season we take chances between life and death,
journey to the infinite limits of ourselves,
with eyes torn from sockets,
into the obscure clouds of hope,
its thunder clangs still bells of our hearts.

My feeling as I just lay here in the dark,
asking myself why I crossed the laws of this land:
because I am much younger than the laws,
because I breathe and am alive,
I can see what is wrong and what is right,
because my hands hold my brother up,

because all I get is lies and slander from law-makers,
and I have a reason to stand respected and steadfast,
for let all the despotic and engineers of evil,
let them form cruel devices and deceive as they will,
will be the hands I crush their arrogant instruments
with!
I see! I have eyes, I have eyes!

I am much younger than the teachings of this land.
You attempt to suppress my tears and laughter,
but no, they come as they come, and if you think me a
lady,
then come and try me; you will find tears and laughter,
can easily turn into the toughest steel imaginable to man.

You have held a trial against me, and found me guilty,
With your polemics and dialectics; but what do I care for
them?
I am a lover and believer of freedom!
I am who I am and I know what I want and need!
If a man suffers he suffers, if a man works he works,
But the way you have it; if a man suffers he does not
suffer,
If a man works he does not work. What is the matter
with you?
Yes, I am ashamed of you, yes, me, I am ashamed of you.
Even as I lay here in the dark, a convicted felon,
on a damp mattress where other felons
have puked their blood and brains out in the night,
where their manly souls have been sodomized by your
chains,
where you have stolen their livelihoods like gutter thieves,
and you wheeze from the rich fat stuck to your ribs.
Friends, I came late into the knowledge of knowing your
true soul and such tardiness helped me escape more of
your torture,
but I will tell you now, from here in the darkness,
I am ashamed of you, yes, me, I am ashamed of you,
and your jailor's keys, your clicking triggers of rifles,
does not scare me; it is your withered heart,

that I stand immune to and ready to defend mine against,
that keeps me awake with pity for you, old, old, old one.

- The intensity of Baca's words show great passion. What do you believe that passion is and why?
- Pull a golden line or phrase that speaks to you from this poem. Use this to begin a poem of your own.
- Use this mentor text and the use of repetition within to create a work of your own.

This first section of the book contains some of the poetry written in Baca's darkest hours of incarceration. His candid and passionate reflections occurred as he fought the demons real and psychological that entered his life. Three excerpts from the letters of Baca and Inman can bring to a close this part of Baca's journey:

> *"I have changed, I am changing. I see things in the air. I must follow, drop my pen for a while, and follow."*　　　*JSB to WI*

> *"You and I have far more in common as poets, bards, shamans than we have differences, and even our differences enrich our relationship with fresh live flavors of being. But what we have in common as poets/shamans—is a huge job of healing and awakening the human spirit…"*　　　*WI to JSB*

> *HEALING EARTHQUAKES! What a vision! Lord, I love you for that one phrase alone—it will revolutionize a whole age. Keep at it, Brother.*　　　*WI to JSB*

Possible Paired Reading:
Healing Earthquakes (2001) Jimmy Santiago Baca

Much like JSB's encounter with the dehumanization process and his journey inward, this section of the book is more heavily scaffolded with ways in which to make sense of the journey. As Baca begins to develop that strong sense of self and self-confidence he uses his supports (correspondence, writing, etc) to enhance his growth, but does not depend on them. This book is set up in the same manner. The second half of this journey will encourage the reader to make connections in a more personal way, leaving the door open for varied expression.

Illuminating
Outward

The hero's journey, should you wish to follow it, continues with some self-realization, and temptations abound within the second half of these readings. Whatever holds power over the individual must be destroyed, literally or figuratively, and one must atone for sins of the past of oneself and/or of the fathers. One must find that inner fulfillment.

It is here that JSB acknowledges the voice he has been developing all along; it is his holy grail. His education is in process, his words and beliefs are actions, and he begins to find balance within incarceration. Learning, reading, and writing provide the "freedom" to live within, yet to illuminate outward.

"I have written well over a thousand poems. They sit in bundles under my bunk; they are my life. I will have to go over them all because in writing them I adhered to no rules or standards, I didn't know any. I know you are busy but I wonder if you could look at more of my poems? I would like to learn from you. I won't be a burden, I just want to learn and be your friend." **JSB to WI**

34
History

The staunchly old White Anglo Saxon Protestants
did a nice paint job
on the house,
but if you scratch the surface
you'll uncover what it hides from us.
We use your history books
to shoo flies away from an old friend's face,
wrinkled and pale as cotton fields we work
but never own,
we tear the pages out
to build fires in our cells
in small tin cans
to heat the coffee up.

- Is history truth?
- Consider the role perspective plays when recording history.
- If you were asked to write the history of your people, what would it say?

Possible Paired Reading:
Texas Tough: The Rise of American's Prison Empire (2010) Robert
Perkinson

> *"I am learning to take situations that beat my body to a
> battered pulp, I am learning to look at myself differently. To
> see the scattered remnants of hopes and dreams, and collect
> them again: return to my old house after the war, pick through
> debris for old photos of the mind and soul; glue together my
> fallen statues of justice and honor, and carefully wrap them in
> my heart for the long trip back. I am learning."*   *JSB to WI*

66
All Day

I have withdrawn and walked in a place
inside myself, trudging across fierce red sands
of my heart,
and through the arroyos, sliding down,
turning over small rocks, patiently, searching
for something to fill me....
I am here: brown body, blood, bones,
sitting in prison on a steel bunk. To Them, I am
found,
tagged with a number, outlawed in Their eyes,
I drag Their chains, I swing Their picks, look long
on Their walls and bars.
I am here to them: my jet black hair, my face, my
kind of eyes
burning
in the yellow straws of sunlight through the bars.
They see my thick forearms, the knife scars that have
cut
my red muscles, busted my bones with steel pipes,
left tiny white gashes at my eyebrows
from the clubs of policemen, to Them, I am here.
To the policemen passing me in patrol cars I am here
To the white farmer with much work and many fields
I am here,

To the heroin addicts and drug dealers I am here,
To them, I am here.
But inside me the lost one I am,
is truly the one Here,
that has been for a thousand
and a thousand years Here,
And on this afternoon, September and sunny,
I hear this deep echo in me, disturb dust gathered in
me,
I hear footsteps on the glacial silence in me,
Leaning his wooly black hair, his ancient brown face,
Across my heart's cave walls, kissing them with lips,
I hear them breathe through the walls in prayer,
scratching my being out with rock,
assembling stones and building a fire in the cave,
intoning my name, across many, many rocky layers,
invoking my presence from out of the mountain of
life I am,
So that sitting on this prison bunk,
I feel fire heaving sharply in me, on a calm American
afternoon,
fire shoots from my tongue, far away from you, in the
desert,
in a prison like other prisons, behind one of those
windows,
black-barred, sparks a birth of beautiful brownness,
Someone else is here, not the image
You imagine passing in your car on the road out
there,
riding, breathing the air I breathe...

JSB speaks to the fire inside of him sparking "a beautiful brownness." What might a fire inside of you spark?

- **Draw a T-chart. On one side, list what others see when they look at you, and on the other, what you see when you look at yourself.**
- **Do the images match?**
- **Think about one thing you'd change about something that appears on either side of the chart and write from the sentence starter, "I am greater than . . ."**

Possible Paired Reading:
One Day in the Life of Ivan Denisovich (1962) Alexander Solzhenitzen

69
I Have Asked and Did Not Receive

I was hungry and jobless
and rejected far too many times,
so I roam my suffering
and travel my anguish,
and offer you gifts of myself,
ones that slipped through your fingers
when you crushed me in your grip,
I have found over miles of lonely
nights in my prison cell, I have found...
like history markers to a free, free land inside.

- When left alone with your own thoughts, to whom or to what do you turn for guidance?
- What gifts might you offer to the world?

"What you're doing with writing is refusing to settle for being just the victim, you're "making room" for real life even there. That is not to say you are placidly lapping up the pain: on the contrary, you just refuse to surrender your spirit to it.
WI to JSB

33
In Pain

This sense of being alone
with my simple self
that hides in fear of being known,
and yet wants to be held close and loved,
sifts like sand through my fingers,
the pain in me gnaws
at my change of clothes to look hip,
to be respected as a gangster,

the pain provokes me
to live careless and fast,
guzzle booze and party,
and tumble madly into the pit of hurt,
exploding and twisted.
I race along the high curves of pride,
seeking shelter in one solitary hand
that has yet to reach out.

JSB speaks to the contradictory nature of being human, to the ways in which we act counter to our true selves to fit in.

- In what ways might pain serve as a catalyst?
- To what or to whom have you reached out?
- What have you offered?
- What does it mean to you to "ride along the high curves of pride"?
- Imagine you are writing a letter to Baca in prison in response to this poem. What would you say?

"There is a change of wind over this land I inhabit, within and without myself. I am living with downright, damnable gangsters, blood spewing cursing madmen, soul curdling violence and brutality, and what is needed is to look straight into the eye of this terrible existence, and then slowly and with the utmost reverence, compose their lives and feelings and loves, and try to adjust my work in quality and depth to their understanding." *JSB to WI*

70
My Experience

One does not forget
the terrible glooms
the rain brings to the soul,
one remembers the years,
the months, the days,
as a time when monsoon rains fell,
wherever it may be, L.A.
or New York, or some dusty little town,

and the streets and windows I stood before,
watching the people pass
in hopes that one of them would be you,
one does not forget the days I was away from you,
through alleys, ghetto tenements, police halls,
through crowds of people in jail cells
where young men laid dying,
every step I took was motivated by love,
looking for you and never finding you...

- For what or for whom do you long?
- In what ways does this longing motivate you?

51
The Little Playground I See

Children running with waving arms,
The cons holding them in their arms,
Or walking with their women
Their arms around their slender waist.
At the end of the visit the cons
Sidled up against the fence
Following after their loved ones
Waving goodbye
As the guard on the gun tower watches.
The cons watch the distracting glints
In the dusk speckle until the car finally disappears.
The playground is empty, the last swing gently dangles
To a stop. Dark claws of shadows spread
Their soothing shade over the little footprints
Of tennis shoes and women's loafers.
The cons leave and pass through a security gate.
The guard frisks them but doesn't find
The pocketful of kisses and warm words
The cons will take out and spread in his hands
Tonight when he goes to bed,
Inspecting each one again and again,
Unfolding the little silk cloth in his heart,
And like diamonds in the moonlight,
Inspect each one again and again.

After reading, "The Little Playground I See"…

- List ways you are connected and/or disconnected.
- Is this important to you? Others around you? Why or why not?
- Is existing in the world easier or more difficult when connected?

68
Silver Water Tower

I remember when I was a child,
on weekends my father and I
drove down to visit my grandmother.
We took the old road, my father himself
had grinded out with others.
He had planted trees alongside the road,
and his face took on a wholesome look,
the history of this land
bright in his brown eyes.
I saw the first sign of the little town,
cuddled against the horizon,
the silver water tower, tall and lank
on steel legs, ESTANCIA, black lettered
across its tank.
Around that tower the link of my blood was unbroken,
thrived solidly in a silver haired woman.

- What does the word "home" mean to you?
- List important people and places in your life.
- Who is the link to your blood?
- Record all of your associations to home in a few paragraphs.
- Re-read what you've written and transform it into a poem.
- Research literature that speaks to a cultural "home" and compare it to the poem.
- Consider an anchoring image for a title, just as JSB did with "Silver Water Tower."

Possible Paired Readings:
The Language of Flowers (2012) Vanessa Dittenbaugh (foster care and more)
Tupac and D. Foster (2008) Jacqueline Woodson (belonging, friendship)
Keisha's House (2007) Helen Frost (survival, home, and more)

18
I Live in Broken Pieces of Myself

Frozen and numb after a long imprisonment,
I slowly return to myself,
My fingers burn clutching the glass tumbler
Of pain, the heritage of an illiterate and poor one,
in my magnitude for searching,
I touched, dipped one finger into the boiling liquid,
Into the glass, into the scalding liquid,
Burning my flesh, putrefaction smoldering
Up to my nostrils, and then,
I clasp the glass tighter,
Wrap my fingers ever and ever tighter around it,
Splintering the glass with a thundering clap
Striking through and through,
And the frozen numb man didn't smile,
But in his eye the faint glimmer of life
Once again fired up,
In this dank dreary cell of hell.
I become a body now, with a mind and spirit,
A heart whose silhouette lies over the earth
With its face to the sun, to the sun.

- Read the poem aloud.
- Re-read this poem silently and mark lines that convey reality with one color and lines that convey hope with another.
- JSB ends the poem with a beautiful image of "A heart whose silhouette lies over the earth / With its face to the sun, to the sun." When you think of yourself as a perfect blend of mind, body, and spirit, what image comes to mind? Capture that image in a graphic interpretation of your choice.

> *"I pause at your beauty, yes, beauty! You man with sneaky dark*
> *eyes you man with bandy legs and black teeth you and you and*
> *you, you with a needle in your arm, a cigarette in your mouth*
> *you with pills in the cupboard you with hunger in your mouth*
> *you with love on your mind you lovers wrapped in sheets all, all*
> *of you I love! Love!"*   *JSB to WI*

44

I Look Around Me

A series of cage doors line prison tiers,
Compartments of signs and furies where we live,
We scream like cougars at the fires of fate,
Once uncut diamonds in these fertile caves,
Now diamonds on the forehead of a rattler,
Striking out at life with its poison, to live,
Without hands or feet or words or heart,
But still with a soul that yearns for freedom.

JSB creates primal imagery of being hemmed in, ready to strike.

- How does this imagery represent Baca's circumstance?
- What would your compartments "of signs and furies" look like?
- In the end, for what or whom might your soul long or yearn?
- What imagery would represent your life?

65
In Prison

In prison the steel doors of my soul crack,
crank open, and sunshine floods through,
down in pin thin light into the darkness
of my heart, in over-pouring beauty,
across the cement floor of my beliefs,
across the steel screens guarding my dreams,

it slowly seeps into the dark bluish heart of mine,
between moist drops of blood,
fierce with needs, fire topped desires.
My pulse flows out like steel rollers
down white lanes of bones, my pulse
filling my body like June apples in a picker's
shoulder bag,
and each apple wanting to be moved, eaten,
held in the hands of someone hungry,
meets only blocks of rock and steel,
and curls hard over the days,
shrivels into itself, squirming,
pinching nerve ends, to a red anger,
tangling tight, hard as plow blades
furrowing the heart with new wounds,
scraping against the bones
like screeching tires around a corner,
wrecking into a wall of prison,
I lie at night, still alive, in my own destruction,
curling hard as shoe leather in my own unseen tears.
They would toss me like an old boot into a junk heap;
but if I am to be a boot, I will walk
about the crumbles, the disturbance,
my lathering of blood washing the face of Death,
scrubbing its hands clean of dirty accusations,
and I say nothing of my cracked life,
the upheaval and destruction,
I walk through it all being someone I never was,
my heels digging into my downfall,
I becoming fully responsible for the future,
I stand in front, my first step toward a new world.

- JSB's pulse flows like steel rollers. What does your pulse flow like?
- What cements your beliefs?
- What screams your dreams?
- What does the word responsibility mean to you and does it change you?
- How does enacting responsibility/behaving responsibly affect those around you?
- Create or find a piece of artwork that "screams your dreams"

Possible Paired Reading:
Life After Death (2012) Damien Echols

> *"Dear Brother, your words are shaman words, sacred, seeing, carrying life and direction."*
> *WI to JSB*

45
Looking

I feel something in me
move—
one movement in particular
crawls out of the dark in me,
a dead hand
on bloody drugged knuckles
unfolding,
coming to life.

To hold in its palm,
lines of my heart's untouched essence,
and the callousness I wear,
when nothing else will light
my path,
or marry them, two separate ones to me.

Life is full of paradox and dichotomies: good-evil, yin-yang, darkness-light. JSB provides a striking image of polar opposites co-existing in one body: a bloody dead hand holding in its palm the heart's untouched essence.

- List some the dichotomies at play in your own life.
- Using this poem as a model, begin the first stanza of your own poem with the words, "I feel" and the second stanza with "To hold."
- After sharing poems in small groups, discuss as a full group why this poem might be viewed as pivotal within the collection.

Possible Paired Reading:
Tattoos on the Heart: The Power of Boundless Compassion (2010)
Gregory Boyle

30
The Push Inward

With society and prison
rubbing me the wrong way,
one pushing me out
and the other pushing me down,
I had no way but to go inward.
Had society or prison taken the time to understand,
It could have been us that changed
for the better, now only me.

- What do the words "social action" mean to you?
- In what ways have you been pushed down or out in your lifetime?
- In what ways have you pushed back? What were the consequences?
- Push back now in your writing about something you feel so strongly about that you wish invite others to join your "call to action."
- Investigate how reading and writing can promote social change. Find a social issue in your community and create a call to action in any media format.

Possible Paired Reading:
Writing for a Change: Boosting Literacy and Learning Through Social Action (2006) National Writing Project, Kristina Berdan, Ian Boulton and Elyse Eidman-Aadahl

> *"I can only grasp myself in a voracious hug, and love love love life in all its merry howlings and screaming horrors! I'll take it all, in my arms, hug each remnant, each dangling odd perspective out of tune with today's thinking, pile it here on my lap, and make me a sweater to keep warm."*   *JSB to WI*

31

A Poem for Me in Prison

I have tasted the fangs of freedom
and its tongue coolly mothering
me where I have erred,
for one like me,
imprisonment is inconceivable.

- What is personal freedom?
- How might one deal with the loss of freedom?
- In what ways might personal freedom have fangs?
- Why might prison be "inconceivable" for JSB?

71

So Blind and Led by the Heat Within

I knew the way I was treated
was deadly wrong,
I took their poison and spread
over my tongue and hands,
the evil was paint and crouched for the kill against
my brothers, the weaker ones...
put a man's eye out...
knifed a few and cracked skulls wide open
for no other reason than to prove I was bad
and to survive the pain of prison.
And then lying in bed one night,
seeing, all the cons around me
walking like empty and distorted images
of someone else they never became,
images to laugh at but no one was laughing,
and my celly that night telling me
about his life, a bare-footed Mexican
who could neither read or write
and gave tourist blow-jobs for enough
money to eat...and so young was he...
Something must be done I said,

and for weeks I tore at myself for an answer,
The answers men lived by were despair and violence,
eventually death…other answers must be found,
not in great books or powerful bureaucracies,
but in me, just me in all this darkness,
like a drop of water sliding off the great block of ice…
In the morning when I woke up
I went to see the counselor
who sat like a pile of dirty dirty clothes
in his wooden chair, slumped and staring at me
with a smirk when I told him I wanted to go
on lock-up…why? I did not know why,
and he thought it was a joke too and thought
once I got over to lock-up I would totally
be shamed and retreat as quickly back into
population.
In lock-up I died a million times,
from shame, from self-doubts of my manhood
from what others thought, I trembled with fear
of what I was doing, stepping out like this
into the greatest darkness I had ever known
for an answer I didn't even know existed, like
flying off the cliff crashing my heart
against the rocks below as I held it in my hands,
a glob of fire flaring with anguish in the night.
I hid myself from the old cons I knew,
averted my eyes and hung my head low,
and one day after filling my tray with food
one of the servers whistled and I blew it,
I turned around and hit him in the face…
the days after that his friends and him
met outside under the stairwell but nothing
happened.
But this is not the way to act I told myself,
you have to be more humble, let them slide;
I soon quit talking to all cons and staff,
and sat by myself through all meals
thinking of an answer for this life of ours,
lost and drunk with spiritual anarchy,
lost my smile, my hair, my weight, and slowly
the man I had been was going away as I began to find

new ways of seeing things, of saying things, and
feeling them;
in my dreams began to flash a light,
or on afternoons sweetened with sunlight
the whole world would flash before me with light,
a brilliant flare inside me would startle me
and outside covering the prison grounds,
prisms of color were flooding over in wild ruckus.
The guards became afraid of me because they
thought
I was crazy and I thought I was crazy too.
I was hated by everyone and everything
and I thought a system totally ran on violence
and oppression, strict power and force in one man,
a defiance to this system was as good a place as any
to start my search for an answer, the best place
of my defiance was at its weakness, and here it was,
a prison within a prison within a prison
and I stood for all it hated, a true beast who would
not march in line with others and work in fields
anymore.
Just realizing my need to be treated like a human
being,
to love myself and the things I stood for, to respect
myself because I loved others, this put a dent
in the great prison system and the cell that would
have held me is dusty and rusty, the fields I would
have worked are overflowing and uncut and my heart
instead of empty and snarling is simple and now
a sanctuary, where I will find the answer I seek...

- In what ways do you go inside yourself?
- What do you seek?
- JSB manages to transform the counselor into a pile of dirty
  clothes. What do you wish to transform in your own life?
  Write a poem expressing that transformation.

*"I realize that just surviving has hardened me tough as plaster. And
I mourn this, because to be human and feel is the greatest fortune
a heart can have. I've barred myself up to keep the wolves from*

attacking, the snakes from entering. I've kept myself from myself
so long I've died. Being dead, you don't feel the humiliation and
brutality of these cemeteries."   *JSB to WI*

7
There Is No Message

There is no message
in those bottles you drain,
nor pity, with your head in hands
as you weep at the kitchen table.
And it does no good
to scream into the telephone.
No one can take sides
for no one has abandoned you
but your own childhood dream of love
that has been torn from you.
From that wound will come
millions of evenings
bringing no one
but the ocean of your silence,
and drowning,
arms out,
you'll call for someone,
Until something changes in you,
and your love becomes
an outdoors holler
between two palms,
that builds upon itself
off the vast loneliness an expanse
between you and other people,
and like a mountainous music
one day you will speak
to someone tuned as you have been tuned,
and in both your voices will sing
of two lost on separate cliffs,
an eagle and its nest.

Alcoholism affected JSB's life in many ways. Many readers will be able to relate to his experience on a personal level; others may need to recall similar situations witnessed in the lives of those around us.

- Although there is "no message in the bottles you drain," JSB does provide advice in the remaining lines.
- Read the poem closely and in your own words, translate his message into a newspaper headline.
- Find a piece of fiction or nonfiction that speaks to the social issue of alcoholism in our society. Pair this with the poem above and write about it.

Possible Paired Readings:
The Absolutely True Diary of a Part-Time Indian (2009) Sherman Alexie
Smashed (2012) Lisa Luedeke
Alcohol abuse, statistics, and help programs can be investigated as well.

3
Home

I have a home, a home, a home,
I felt when I left it at once,
Like a skeleton in wind,
without flesh or fullness.
I felt light with adventure in my boots,
and further and further away
I was home,
all the distance my eyes could reach,
could not replace the larger thoughts,
whether I had closed the door for good,
if the seeds I planted would grow...
Niches and recesses in my bulge of new freedom,
where lie old family jewels and secrets
like old withered scrolls,
and what I had left behind in the cave of my beginning,
a coiled rope I climbed the cliffs with,
and gently dropped myself into new understanding,
chisels of wishful thinking now in the dust,

to rust in the cloudburst of their regret.
Myself out here now, my breathing
carving out a hope of warmth and love,
against the anonymous air of the city,
with its windows strung with plastic green vines,
and little neon signs and advertisements.
I feel myself growing more human with every mile,
almost like a child that wants to run
from the dark to his mother.
Whether I should cry from sadness or joy,
the sun tells it all, so the grass does also.
I am a pilgrim in my own small way,
and have come to see people and places,
enshrined in my thoughts,
that glow in the dark of my home,
when I talked to them there, bending over
among the clay pots or wrung rags on the sink
faucets,
they would whisper, come come come...
Home is home base, homeboy for the men,
the cue to bet big or don't come at all,
who play the game of life. Home is the place
where you can place your finger on the hole in the
dam,
and save the day. It is the place where hurricanes
sleep
in old photographs and roses in old boots and
slippers.
It gives us reason to go and come, go around and
around,
Like rings in an old wooden tree,
that preserve memoirs and sweet years and roots,
as our limbs slowly begin to creak, and young ones
fly to our laps as if nests.

- What do you run toward?
- What do you run from?
- List regrets you've had in your life up to this point.
- Now choose one regret and re-write the ending to reflect a different outcome.

"Fire is all within me, warmth run down my fingers, pours from my eyes, under the cold rough blankets of flesh of my friends around me."   *JSB to WI*

14
Who Will Give Me Eyes

The wind outside whistles
and throws sand through the window
into my cell, the night flood lamps
wobble, the wind thrashes against
the coiled bob-wire on the walls
and gun towers...
I am lonely for her warm hands,
beneath my blankets my legs shiver,
my whole body is hot in a fever of loneliness,
emotions gush forth raw and immense,
they crash against my heart
like great icebergs,
in a sea of boundless sensation,
unable to retrieve her warm hands,
in my profusion of feelings
the wind outside I choose as my eyes,
and suddenly everything is quiet
and it takes me to her warm hands...

- JSB personifies the wind in this poem. Read it carefully and use different colored pencils or markers to highlight all of the various sensory perceptions he uses.
- In small groups, complete this sentence. The wind is Baca's _____. Find evidence from the text to support your answer.

23
So, Lovely Lady

Have I scared you in some way?
If so, just think for a moment,
ponder upon the simplicity of life
for a moment, the beauty of just being you,
and just being me, of just understanding
how our lives have been,
filled with sorrow and love, endurance and
achievement,
no matter the social hierarchy,
that you wear silks and live by the sea,
that you wear diamonds and perfumes,
and I rough cloth and work boots and jeans,
and my hair tousled by sandy desert winds;
hearts and souls and minds cannot be confined
just to these, they must dream and yearn,
then they are alive and real,
they pass the planes and pretensions,
the structure of poverty and wealth,
and spring into each other's days,
like beams of moonlight through tree boughs at night,
shuddering the leaves alive,
silly whims float away, true feelings blossom,
and believe in love, in communication with the world.
Ponder, upon simplicity of life for a moment...

- If you lost all of your material trappings, what would be left to make you happy?
- Write a few paragraphs including specifics about why those things would be your source of happiness.

Possible Paired Reading:
Gift from the Sea (1955) Anne Morrow Lindbergh

60
My Ears

My ears have become rusty locks
as guard voices rattle and jangle
in them like ancient skeleton keys.
Next they take axes to my heart
but still it will not give.
Inside they hear a man laughing
and think he is mad.
I smile at them like a Houdini,
it's all magic,
to escape the henchmen and environment
of hate and brutality,
out of this crude box I jump
and smile at my own death.
In the twilight seeping through each crack
walking down between bunks with sleeping men,
like un-blossomed buds on a dark green vine
their white sheets like hoar frost,
their rough blankets like dying petals
folded up around their heads,
tangled and sprawled, they were seeds
ready to grow, but winter came early.
The faces,
remind one of graphs: bad years and good ones,
strict lines running across them.
Many of them have no education.
Impulsive
as a kitten's paw for a ball of thread,
tangling themselves up inextricably
in wild gardens, guarded
pruned by prison shears,
until they are brittle stalks
and dead clumps of fallen things.
I try to find something positive
in prison life. Friendships are rare,
except with TV's and homosexuals and shanks.
Sincerity becomes a commodity,
delivered and trucked through little dark alleys
of the soul at night, a top secret explosive

ignited by the smallest smile.
It becomes a war to stay human. You see
guards each minute of the day, and remind
yourself what you were, and fight just to believe,
just to believe you can go back to a normal life
someday.
A man loses himself sometimes, after many years
in prison, after too many walls and barbwire fences,
he sits alone sipping coffee, talking with friends
about who got stabbed last night:
he will not allow himself to think
about a good life.

JSB speaks to the ebb and flow of losing oneself and finding oneself.

- Collectively, what threatens our humanity?
- Individually, what, if anything, threatens your own?

"And now, I strike against the violence with violence, gave them another scar, another reason to strike out at a lesser smaller man, savagely indent a human face, put teeth up through cheeks as they pummel the loose dazed human head… not I shall not strike anyone, only if struck at the heart, and I shall strike back by understanding my opponents, by betraying their wish for me to involve myself violently in their game, I will not raise a hand. I will strike at them with peace. Is that it, Afternoon? Peace? Peace when I have it buried deep in me, uncover it, offer peace to them, when I don't have it? Carve out these rocks of hate clogged against my soul, and find in them a subtle vein running against the grain, and stand on that grain? Give it my full sincerity, take the speck as my altar…I will try, I am convinced I will win."   *JSB to WI*

21
To Be Worth Something

Outside the prison a mile out,
on a small hill the Army has war games.
You can hear the booms! boom! boom!
shudder the solitary air of prison.

Guards on catwalks along the walls,
hear the rifle shots and boom! boom!
The main yard whistle gives a whistle
Hoooo! Hoooo! Hoooo! Hoooo!
A blaring tribute for another shifty,
as new guards walk along the catwalks,
carrying their lunch pails and rifles,
slung over their shoulder like infantrymen.
Back from the war, without a job,
their hands alienated from plough and shovel,
eating government food, wearing government clothes,
issued government rifles, and paid by the
government,
They stand watch over their brothers and sisters,
who think and reacted to their environment,
who took dope to forget that everything was wrong,
who broke laws that did not speak for them.
Yes there's a war on. It's between the living,
and the dead, between those who feel and do not feel,
between those who give in and those that do not,
and victory is life itself, life for humans.
Humans, whose weapons are endurance and hope,
the robbers, the killers, the drug users,
knowing they are down, somehow keep fighting,
to do right, to show themselves as they really are,
and they have come into your camp
with a flag of peace, and they were torn to shreds.
You want no peace, but want to make men into game,
and chase them down with dogs and mobs.
But no more: you will not even give us a chance.
The few that try, are shot in the back.
So we are kept in cells, twelve-inch thick walls of
rock,
three inch steel doors with guards everywhere.
To want freedom is ok. But to fight for it is not.
The question is freedom, that is the question,
that's what it's all about today in prison
that's what it's all about everywhere,
to be worth something, to be free humanly,
to be worth something, to be free humanly.

- What defines your humanity?
- What threatens to take it away or diminish it?
- What are your "weapons" to preserve and protect it?
- What does it mean to be free?
- Read a primary source document that speaks of the subject of freedom. Compare that primary source document to JSB's poem above. Compare and contrast the two works and use evidence from both texts.

56
That Time You Left

When you left, mama,
When I escorted you
To the airport,
A baggage boy carrying your heart,
Leaving you in line with it
As you stood to board the plane,
I sensed what was coming on.
The minute you left I descended
The stairs and strode down
The long and narrow tunnel,
People glancing at me
As I reached the end of the tunnel,
Ascended the stairs
And stepped stolidly into the lobby,
Scattered with busy people
Peering at me as they passed.
The people that looked at me
Knew it was my heart that hurt.
I was thinking of you,
And without glancing at anyone
Briskly went out of the airport.
I had been crying all along.
That feeling of not caring
Has been with me since then,
Following me in all I do
Like warm hands
At each door that opens to me.

- In what ways can you personally connect to these lines and images?
- Think about the words parents, love, and abandonment. Can they simultaneously inhabit someone's world? In what ways?

46
Padre

I have your eyes and hands.
You were driven away father
and knew not how to plead for redemption.
You were a hunter in the wilderness
of shadows. You painted your name on rocks.
You painted the legends of our people
driven from their land. Children are hungry,
watching the new freeway being built
where their fields once were.
Little flowers that grow around rocks
tended by nature was your joy father.
And the silence that sunk into the barren night,
When travelers have reached their homes,
A funeral silence, silence resurrecting
from the rocks, like a procession
of dead popes and philosophers,
king of a silent world,
was the way my father talked to the world.
He was drunk with untamed sensations,
he worked every day with shoes,
fitting them to feet like a scientist
carefully pouring liquids in gold cups.
He worked with bones and flesh and blood,
he knew leather polished and smooth,
he knew the gold and silver buckles,
so when children or grown ups
came to buy a shoe from him,
he could go into the shoe room
in the back, pull a special box out,
and lay the shoes before the young eyes
like dreams come true.

The shoe room glowing with rich scents
of whiskey, of leather and sweat,
a silvery musky taste in the air,
like a garden
where a king lived and roamed
for fifty years giving flowers
to the young and old alike.
Mi Padre! The color of dark clay
with eyebrows dark as olives!
The town was once filled with laughter,
now no more. The trees you planted,
to give shade to the farm workers,
a white farmer made his and put a fence there
so you could not touch them anymore.
Memories of when life was good,
made you stagger drunkenly into the night,
your heart trembling in your fingers
that tipped the bottle to your lovely lips,
as the whiskey poured down your throat
like acid burning the eyes of yesterday
as glowing as the sun in alfalfa fields.
You were trying to kill the meaning of life!
A life diminished and without strength,
a life without arms or legs
that made people crawl on bellies,
a life without hands to work the earth
and create beautiful shoes for the people,
was no life to you. Only a suffering,
a broken body parched for the past
like drought stricken clay
where corn no longer tall and straight
and free in the wind and sun.
The whiskey trickled down your throat
bleaching your mind white with numbness.
And you don't care anymore
when I saw you crying sitting on a tree stump,
cursing from withered lips like winter tree-boughs
dropping their dead leaves,
from lips that kissed my mother once,
a green eyed woman soft and surprisingly beautiful,

a secret book bowered with dark-leaved trees,
with fingers and legs supple as grass stems
swaying in sunlight the first day of spring.
No more—now in the cold marble rooms of your
heart
you walked, burning photographs and letters,
leaning your head against the black rock
with the wind to your face, solitary soldier,
repenting for a heart too strong and loving,
a relic of a lost and broken life.
But how was it, papa? As long as you lived,
no one knew you. You fought the calloused world
in the afternoon soaking up your energy to continue
your life and cleanse your thoughts.
What it was that killed you no one knew,
but in your mind the blood popped,
burst like a bottle in the fire
as the slivers of glass struck my eye
and I wept like ivy on your coffin.
Your voice comes to me in dreams.
I have a picture of you and me,
and I am sitting on your knee, you are smiling,
secretly and young, your arms around me,
and I am wearing new shoes.
Ah papa, you fell on the battlefield.
You didn't want to teach me
that some things are worth dying for,
you wanted me to be a soft prince.
But look, papa... I too have listened and heard
The spirits crying for me,
and look, papa... I found your heart pounding
in the waves of their passing,
beat against the rocks of the mountain's brow,
in the bells that sing each Sunday from the church,
in the yellow panting tongue of the sun.
I too have held the pain inside,
thinking we never talked to each other,
there were things you didn't want me to know
about your life,
but papa, I know, and I love you still.

You were no stranger, for where you went,
I followed secretly, and saw, yes I saw,
how you wept and bled. I touched the red drops
and felt the warmth of your soul.
I knew that none so bad as you, none,
not those that promised us good schools,
not those that promised us justice,
not those that promised to give the old ones medicine,
not those that promised to give us decent wages,
was our land, none of these with their manners,
none of these, wanted to give me
a good life so bad as you did, a good life.
But papa, in your ragged sorrow, in your chains
of guilt, in your drunken and violent nights,
have given me the truth! hear me, papa, wherever
you are!
You have given me what I need to live with,
and I cannot name it, but when I see a brown child
smile,
a little girl tie her hair into braids,
a horse chewing alfalfa in the sunshine,
when I see two old ladies leaving church,
when I see old men lean against the bar,
when I see the trees blow at the air their leaves,
when I pass bars and see putas in short skirts
or hear the whine of a small puppy,
or hear the barn doors thud against the wind,
I think of you and something in me rejoices,
for we struggle, we fail and win,
but we are not who they want, but we are who we are,
and will always remain so even
the drunks downtown or the Chicanos in universities,
the Chicanos that don't know how to speak Spanish,
all of us, we know we are who we are—
Papa we are not dreamers anymore, we are rising,
los Latinos—with men like you papa who told us
little,
in the silence we heard you, a wounded animal,
quiet and fearless, hunted by lawmen,
do you hear me papa? Things are changing…

- When you think no one is watching, how do you behave?
- How do you nurture empathy for yourself and others?
- How did your parents leave their mark on you?
- What mark to you wish to leave on your children or the future?

Rehumanization
Process

"No! I am the kink in doom's link! It is I, that when the chain passes over the wheel, I shall knot up the machine, and burst the hold! Stop the machine; take the chain and round and round and round will I swirl it and finally fling it away into oblivion, away into some clump of wild grass, to decompose, rise from earth again, as I have. That is why I speak as I do."

JSB to WI

52
Pushed Into a Corner

Put into a corner, punished, put into a black hole,
I bring my sense together like rocks
And spark the flame, the wing of light,
That burns through their documents of my guilt.
Their accusations are fantasies, with no earthly weight
That ties them to earth where I am,
They are outside of myself, hung like effigies,
Slandered, ridiculed, beaten with club tongues
The documents of my guilt give you nothing but hate.
Here I am, in touch with sensuality
Given between people in love,
My hands bleed, my knees bleed, because I choose
To stay in touch with it, with humans clutching each other.
If I violate rules, I must.

- Have you ever been pushed into a corner, either literally or figuratively? If not, perhaps you have witnessed someone else being pushed in this way. Write about how you or the other person reacted at the time.
- Re-write a more positive result. What would it look like? Be as specific as possible.

54
Little Sparrow

Fraternal pagan, fearless,
pecking at the dark padlocks
in my heart,
as I awake your recital.
Before the lights go on,
I lay on my bunk and listen to you:
my face is chipped and scarred
like the carved bust of Julius Caesar
fallen in decay and dust,
draped with a sheet in these prison tombs.
To the world I have fallen!
But you little sparrow, you are still
my faithful friend, as I sit here
on this balcony of darkness,
you dance of freedom.
I toss you crumbs hard as coins
from my breakfast plate,
and toast you with my first cup of coffee.
Then you give a loud sharp note,
like a trumpeter before the battle
that each day is in prison:
again I toast you with my cup of coffee
as you flutter out the cracked broken glass
of the window.

JSB often includes images of the sparrow in his poetry. Research the possible meanings of the sparrow and re-read the poem with new understanding.

- **When seeking refuge, most often people find it in another human being. Imagine seeking refuge and solace in the natural world. Create a scene using as many sensory perceptions as possible.**

35
Early Morning

In streams of sunlight,
my soul,
bulged with breath
brightly thudded against the light
and heard the grass laugh,
the old roots gulp,
sore throated and huffing,
from lack of water and poison soil.
Shallow hearts tittering
in their fancy paper lives,
thieves and bandits in civil office,
sickle-tooth smiles,
chisel away trust in life.

- Can you recall a time, place, or situation when your entire
  being felt especially alive and vibrant, when your soul
  "bulged with breath"? First take time to respond freely and
  quickly in writing, then mine your own words for a poem
  that captures that feeling.

28
To This Hour

I whisper to the night, to the broom
to the fan, to my grumpy typewriter,
to the mirror, the yellow wastebasket,
the toilet, all the books I read,
the bars of this cage, my dirty towels
and house slippers wound with shoestrings
and Elmer's glue, I whisper to the rumpled sheets
and coarse woolen blanket, the cold floor,
I whisper to all things in my life,
that it has been impossible for me
to love anyone but you.

- Make a list of inanimate objects in your life to which you
  might whisper a secret or some bit of amazing news.
- Hold one of those objects in your mind and image how it
  might respond.

29

The Morning

Suddenly a golden throng,
of thorns shot up to the sky.
They were breathtaking,
a suffusion of tremendous splendor,
of immaculate radiation
blinding the heart,
and the SUN-CROWN rose
like a gold diamond,
exploding and bursting...
the sky was smooth
and beautiful china blue,
I walked so delicate
in the roaring hush,
in the soft blonde undulations
of the Sun,
rippling on the walls of my cell
as my soul dovetailed on horizons a million miles
away…

JSB uses a sun crown as the central image of this poem. Think about your favorite time of day.

- **What fresh image can you create to convey your love for this particular time?**
- **Write a poem that pays homage to this time of day using your own fresh controlling image as the poem's anchor.**

42
In My Isolation

My thoughts resist the future and past
For they offer curious sufferings,
A type one should not confront till death.
Life was a gift for me.
Sometime ago, simple and primitive
In its beauty. I nourished it

And held it close to my heart.
Dreams mount up in me,
The aging gray winds of the past
Gust against the grimy windows
Of the present time,
Cracking into a million pieces
Like rain I want to catch
But don't know where to begin,
The earth shudders under the thunder.

This poem speaks to the many dreams JSB had, so many he didn't know where to begin.

- What dreams do you hold?
- How can you catch them?
- Journal about one dream. Include steps you must take to realize it.

36
Changes

They will come my friends,
all the hardships and empty promises,
the small things we live with daily,
are only slopes that train our legs
for higher mountains ahead.
Dimly reflected in our souls,
are the old songs of our forefathers and mothers,
half-moon mirrors coming back on our lips,
drowning the deceptive words of tricksters,
breaking the clickety-clack of their lies.
I hear the open roar of our freedom coming,
the aromas of freedom flood the darkness
with incense and blowing fires,
smoke out the snickering corporate hyenas
blind with self-pity and apathy.
The music of dark rain
reaches into something
man calls a dream.

JSB transmutes hardships and empty promises into "slopes that train our legs to climb higher mountains ahead."

- **What are some of the obstacles in your life?**
- **Can you create an image that conveys how you might navigate over, around, or under them? How will the materials you use help to portray that image?**

37
No Prison Can Keep Me from You

Prosecutors shackle me with white lies,
guards squat in a cage and bury the key,
racists tear my love into bits and scraps,
goon squads shove my face against the bars,
and pat me down, but they do not understand
that my heart is a cutting torch,
melting the bars and shackles and snapping the chains,
dissolving the doubts that flash through your eyes,
file down the bitter teeth of betrayal,
that eat at your heart with my kisses,
uproot drip-like ratted vines of Materialism,
that envelope and thorn around the heart.

JSB's heart is a cutting torch in this poem.

- **What might your heart become as a source of power?**
- **How might this image help you achieve your heart's desire?**
- **What prevents you from living the life you image for yourself?**
- **What small steps might you take to change the course of your future?**

"I must write this afternoon. Oh how I have changed! The afternoon is such a blessing!"   *JSB to WI*

57
Winter Morning

Cool air seeps in through the black grill
of my cell, cool streams of air like pennants
fluttering from the castle walls,
soft as a little girl's hair.
Through the grime-sodden windows
cracked by sparrow's beaks,
unto my cheeks the freshness streams.
Grounded into this prison life,
each ounce of me, rolled and flattened,
thrown on the hot grill of my anger,
the morning air comes like mountain water
into my lungs as dusty as flour, thickened
with bits of blue and green dawn-sky
savory as hot chili dappled with dew,
just picked from the garden.
Sweet life! Wondrous and beautiful!
Let me button my coat quickly
and go into the mist and smoke of the somber
compound.
Let the church bells jangle,
trample the dawn with vibrant hooves.
I want to go walk about this morning,
on roads with trees brown with happy trunks.
Doves sputter in startled clouds above.
I look deep and am mesmerized by beauty of life!
Sweet life! Wondrous and beautiful!
Don't expect me to walk without a large voice
or walk in a laggard's gait.
I talk with the subtle explosiveness of roots,
the sharp and silver tongues of waves;
I lick the sun like a lion licking its paw,
and grumble good naturedly through the morning,
with stride-full excitement, strong emotion,
with a sureness toward life!
Taps of hammers break,
recede and rise rhythmically,
rhyming with the pulsations of early workmen,

people's names are called out into the street,
yellow busses groan and rattle up to their stops,
and the sun curls golden, flares open...
Sweet life! Wondrous and beautiful!
Lips still warm with dreams, young women
braiding their hair...
no, don't expect me to walk calmly in this,
no, I sing sore-throated in a trance.
My joy is thick as goat milk that pours across my
tongue.
My love is rich as coffee that awakes the traveler in me.
O winter sun! Whistling at the ladies with the workmen
Such a deep strong colorful life!
Happy with hands in my coat pocket, I stand on the
corner and watch.
Sweet life! Wondrous and beautiful!

- Write one word that conveys the mood of this poem.
- Re-read the poem and jot down every word or image that
  supports this mood.
- If you were to write a poem about your life at this moment
  in time, what one word might convey it's mood? Write that
  poem.

41
Day Is Beauty

Beauty is in the day, day is beauty, day
Day, day, even when you say it,
doesn't it make you smile, day.
Then let us breathe deeply day this day deeply
breathe and shudder in its delight...
All plants breathe with us, there is a chorus of life,
breathing life, day. Then let us go calmly, for we are,
everything and every day is us, smile, sing, do not be
afraid,
listen to me sing...day I breathe, yes,
what a wonderful song is breath praising day.

- Use either word you chose for the previous exercise to write a short poem that plays with language and repetition as JSB does here with "day" and "beauty."

Possible Paired Reading:
Who Will Know Us? (1990) Gary Soto

53
When You Look at the Rain

The sun, the rocks, the trees, or see men working on a
house, Run your fingers through the saw-dust,
Hear the crackle of mountain twigs
      In the wind,

Smell the water as she weeps
And sinks through the seasons,
Listen to young leaves in prayer
Unfold themselves like palms
      Of a preacher,

Brown and old as earth,
Listen how the bells toll
At the new night's birth
As twilight rubs on adobe walls
      Her holy ashes,

Blessing the village before sleep,
Each ebbing ring slides into her cup
Of sherry wine as sparrows and doves
Fly one last time above,
      This is what I love.

JSB embraces life and all it has to offer.

- What does life offer you and how do you embrace it?
- What do you see when you "look at the rain"?
- Address the nature of personification in this text.

*"I will carry my vision to you and if you kick me in the groin,
I will understand you. I will be silent and if you threaten me,
I will give you my shoes if you ask for them. Don't think I
am weak. I want to give them to you. I am sure of beauty and
giving, oh you know I am so sure, so wonderfully secure in this
little bit of wisdom, I will give you everything I have, because
there is beauty in this, and I want beauty, in you in me, in us."*

JSB to WI

*"You are not wasting your life where you are; painful as
it is you are doing a deep and necessary work, and it is
recognized by at least some of us in this world. Please don't
ever underestimate yourself or the strategic place you're in
to generate healing and meaning, the two main ingredients
needed for us to grow whole in this time. Sometimes things
have a way of happening when you <u>let</u> them and that you,
yourself, <u>are</u> not being forgotten and <u>will</u> <u>not</u> be forgotten."*

WI to JSB

59
I Keep Thinking How Beautifying Life Is

With all the rot and death
around me,
I feel overwhelmed
by life's beauty.
So much, I get ear aches and heartaches.
I feel like an adventurer
crossing a river,
in my hands I carry life,
through silence cold as ice,
through violence and bloodshed and despair,
I carry life in my hands,
and there is nothing like it.
To carry means
all things are prepared for my touch,
all things can be tempered,
and felt until they are understood,
and the struggle it demands of me,

I love, I believe in,
and test those beliefs
with my body and soul and heart,
not blatantly test them,
but by understanding,
blend them into the coarse and gritty palm
of the world,
overpower its destructive and angry fist
with my humanity, tenderness, endurance.
Life is so beautiful.

Imagine that your words represent colors on an artist's palette.

- **What words do you hold in your hands at this stage in your life?**
- **List as many words as you can that possess special meaning for you.**
- **Now put them on your palette and paint a poem with the words you carry and blend them until you achieve the hue that reflects you in this moment in time.**

Possible Paired Reading:
The Things They Carried (1990) Tim O'Brien

This brings us to the end of Baca's poems, but certainly not to the end of thought associated with them. If you were reading for pleasure, go back, read your favorite or the one that evokes the most emotion in you. Think about how you, the individual, can make a difference.

If this is being used for education purposes, writing workshops, or for your own journaling and response, the following are activities that offer some degree of choice when looking at the entire collection of poems.

Cross-Curricular Connections

- Invite participants to select two poems from each section for a total of eight and search for pieces of music that reflect the essence of each. For each selection, participants write a paragraph or two to justify the reasons why they believe the music aligns with the each poem.
- Talented musicians might create an original piece of music that interprets the entire collection: dehumanization, spiraling inward, illuminating outward, and rehumanization.
- Dancers could create an original piece of choreography based upon the four sections.
- Invite students to select one poem from each section to use as a springboard for the creation of a mandala, with one poem interpreted in each quadrant. Mandalas generally have a highly defined center, which students are free to create as the focal point.
- Invite students to create a radio play or video based upon selected works in this collection.
- Invite architectural or drafting students to create a new, more humane prison design. In order to complete this project, they will need to research current prison design. The final design should include a paper that speaks to the changes they made and how they view each one as more humane.
- Most prisons today minimize the use of technology by inmates. After researching the practices in their state or local prison, invite students to write a persuasive essay (or an argumentation paper) attempting to convince officials to allow inmates greater access to contemporary technologies.
- Invite students to develop a money-saving proposal for their local prison. With guidance, the instructor could help students to forward promising ideas to prison officials for consideration.
- Invite students to create a large poster that primarily features statistics to tell the story of their state's prison system.
- Invite students interested in wellness to research the nutrition and health and fitness practices of their local system and to make recommendations to improve some aspect of one or the other, or both.
- Invite students interested in medicine to research the current system used by their state to treat physically or mentally ill prisoners. This can be focused on current and/or past systems.

- Look at the research on foreign prisons outside of your own country. How do they differ. How is language and/or culture a barrier for communication and presenting one's case to the courts?
- Advanced language classes could provide a written translation of one of Baca's poems and write to explain how translating into another language may lose some of the author's intended nuances.
- Create an artist representation of one or more of Baca's poems. A written piece of explanation or reflection could accompany the piece.
- Invite a student whose first language is Spanish to translate one of Baca's poems and read it aloud to others to provide a cultural connection.
- Look at the later works of Baca and compare and contrast the style and tone of these poems to those of poems or works written in later years.
- How does Baca's hero's journey teach the reader the value of literacy?

Sheehan & VanBriggle:
On a Personal Note

Reflections on America

Denise VanBriggle

Welcome to America, home to 5% of the world's people and 25% of the world's prisoners.   ~NAACP

These words appeared in my Facebook newsfeed recently, thanks to the NAACP, and I immediately shared them with everyone in my social network. The truth is, I am fortunate to live among those who live freely; however, I also realize that a variety of circumstances could instantly shift me into the unlucky percentage of individuals who live behind bars. Perhaps a poor decision translates into a DUI, or a quick text message translates to involuntary manslaughter. When I became a prison volunteer, I attended a mandatory orientation program during which the Corrections Officers kept emphasizing, inmates are just like you. Just like me. Those words still resonate.

I am Troy Davis. I am also each attentive man who sat before me in a prison reflective writing group. I am several of my former high school students who walked slowly past the prison classroom window, eyes downcast, hoping I would not recognize them. I am Gino, the inmate who trained my cell dog, Izzy, and with whom I have been corresponding since 2003. And I am my dear friend, Jimmy Santiago Baca, who served 5½ years in prison in the 70s and who taught himself to read and write while incarcerated. He is a role model for everyone who dwells in the land of "I can't" or "I won't" because he rose above all obstacles and became an internationally acclaimed writer after his release.

In August of 2011, I began co-facilitating a men's writing group at the local prison with Dr. Irene Baird of Pennsylvania State University. Dr. Baird is the person who first introduced me to Jimmy Baca through his compelling memoir, *A Place to Stand*, in 2005. She recommended that Gino and I read the memoir together, and without wanting to sound overly dramatic, it is a book that changed both of our lives. For me, it re-ignited a social justice fire that had been smoldering in my soul since the 1970s. (I can still vividly remember writing a persuasive paper for my Problems of Democracy class in which I argued for the abolition of the death penalty.) For Gino, it gave him a sense of hope that one day he, like Jimmy, will be able to transcend his wrongdoings and make a life for himself outside the prison walls when he is released in 2016. He entered prison a young man and will leave a man who many would consider past his prime.

When I began co-facilitating the men's writing group, I remember feeling that all of my life experiences had provided a clear footpath to that very moment in time. I flashed back to 1974 when Patricia Quann, then the director of the Pennsylvania Commission on Crime and Delinquency, took me to tour the Camp Hill Correctional Facility. At the time I was working in the office of Governor Milton Shapp and had not yet turned nineteen. I can recall the visit as if it were yesterday. We walked across the parking lot on a crisp autumn day and the leaves rose in colorful cyclones on the black macadam before us. After making our way through security, I distinctly remember the sharp contrast between the breeze outside and the stillness of the air inside. It was as if we had entered a tomb. We walked through cell block after cell block and I recall how surprised I was that many of the men had televisions and radios, and what in my naïve experience seemed to be far more than I expected to find. On the ride back to the Governor's Office, I remember asking Ms. Quann the purpose of all of those creature comforts, and she said it helped keep the inmates occupied and easier to control. I understood.

Then I flashed back to 1994, when I was invited by the Pennsylvania Council of the Arts to judge and edit a large collection of poetry submitted by inmates from correctional facilities across the Commonwealth of Pennsylvania. For days on end, their words transported me inside their hearts and minds, and I longed for the day the depressing project would come to an end. I was not in prison, yet I felt their confinement in every poem I read, and there were hundreds and hundreds of them. Their words, coupled with the footage of all of the prison films I had ever seen, became my idea of incarceration in America. And it was not a pretty reality.

And then my mind reached back to 2003 when I first met my prison pen pal at a correctional facility in Virginia. As I mentioned earlier, he trained my cell dog, Izzy, and I traveled to the prison to attend her graduation ceremony. Gino and I became fast friends, and much of what I know about life on the inside can be attributed to him. He always talks about how much he has learned from me, but I have learned as much from him. In addition to training dogs, he earned his journeyman's and master electrician certification in prison and helps to teach his trade to other inmates. He was asked to keynote at the prison graduation ceremony at which he received his professional certificates. I know he viewed this as a tremendous honor, this opportunity to speak before his peers. To give you a small taste of our friendship and to reveal a bit about what is weighing heavily on his mind these days, I want to share with you a few excerpts from our most recent exchange of letters:

Gino, October 11, 2011

I want to tell you how thankful I am to have you as a friend and for showing me that I "matter" too. The fact that you still write to me after 8 years is enough proof that you think about me and that I am worth your time. I have learned to cherish this gift of yours and see its value in my life. But I owe you so much more than just a simple gesture of gratitude and thanks. You seem to really see great potential or something in me because you make me part of your life or your day and you share me with others. I am extremely touched that you tell people about me and our friendship. For a very long time I felt awful about the person I had become and the crimes I have committed. I know people don't like criminals because we make the world a dark place to live. I don't want to be hated or thought of as a man that brings about darkness. I want to be liked, I want to be seen as a man that builds a better world and brings light, happiness, and joy to others. Most of all, I want to be a man that is forgiven. Because you see something in me, believe in me, and share me with others . . . you are the bridge that connects me to others so that I can have the opportunity to be forgiven.

The professor from Canada, Leona English, was very kind with her words about my writing and, yes, they did brighten my day and my spirit. . . . Your friend Penny Alsop also gets my sincerest gratitude and thanks because she has been gracious enough to allow me and my writing to be a part of her Great Big Crazy Love website with you.

I want you to know, Denise, that whatever greatness my life achieves, you were and are instrumental in making it happen and I hope the world recognizes your part—you, see, I'm not the only one building a better world, you are too!

Gino, October 11, 2011

I really hope that my life will be meaningful and not just functional when

I get out. I don't want to just go to work and pay bills, you know? I want to give, be of service. I have been thinking about Jimmy Baca and I wonder when he was in prison, sitting in the dungeon (the hole) learning to read and write, writing his poetry. . . I wonder if he saw then where his life is now. I think about that all the time. Where/what will my life be 2-3 years after I get out? Baca had his poetry and love for reading and writing to give him a vision and a purpose. I think about what I have to offer. Of course, I think I'm a really good electrical instructor and I'm really knowledgeable about the field. But I also have an incredible story. I know I'm in my mid-forties now and will be almost 50 when I'm released, but I don't think I need youth on my side to use my life to help others. I think my story should be told and if it is, it will be a grand example of success. I want people to know that regardless of how deep we bury ourselves in mistakes and trouble, there is always hope and always success if you want it. I want people to know that criminals can change and be reformed, regardless of how hopeless it seems. I've been in and out of jails and prisons all my life and I found a way to change—of course, I'll have to show everyone once I'm out that I won't come back! But you get what I mean. I guess those are the two main things I have to work with as far as a vision is concerned, are my electrical skills and my story. I wonder if these are enough and if they will be of use.

Denise, October 25, 2011

Please don't think I have forgotten about you . . . I haven't! There are several important reasons why I haven't written, but I will share those you a bit later in this very long letter. First I want to say CONGRATULATIONS on earning your Environmental Protection Agency certification for refrigerants. Another feather in your cap, my friend. All of your hard work will better position you for employment post-release, Gino, and your efforts will pay off. Don't ever question why you are doing what you do. If my memory serves correctly, you are to be released in January of 2016, which is soon to be just four years away! I know you talked about the routine getting hard in your most recent letter, but think about how far you've come. Pretty amazing progress in the years we've been writing to one another! You asked me for the address of The North American Board of Certified Energy Practitioners (NABCEP). It is 56 Clifton Country Rd., Suite 202, Clifton Park, NY, 12065. I hope you can get all of the information you need to be certified as a Photovoltaic installer. Not sure what that is, but it sounds impressive. Good luck.

So, you have your trade and certifications and you have your stories, both of which will sustain you after your release. I plan to share your last two letters and this response with Penny. Perhaps they will find their way to the Great Big Crazy Love website, who knows. I do believe your words can help others, just as Jimmy Santiago Baca's words have helped you. Since my retirement, I am volunteering at the local prison and am currently co-facilitating a reflective writing workshop for men. The first book the men read was A Place to Stand *and the second was* Up From Here *by Iyanla VanZant. If you read the VanZant book, let me know what you think. I'd be interested in your perspective. It is a quick read but, like Jimmy's memoir, begs to be dipped back into every now and then. Did you ever read Jimmy's semi-autobiographical book of poetry* Martin and Meditations on the South Valley? *I just re-read it two weeks ago and think you would like it, too.*

I don't think I mentioned in my last letter that A Place to Stand *is being made into a documentary film. I've been helping with the fundraising campaign, especially with large corporations. All of the interviewing has been completed, and it promises to be an amazing piece of work when it is finished. The director and producer have interviewed so many interesting people from the DEA agent who was shot to some of Jimmy's cellies and friends, like Bonafide. I can't wait to see the finished product. Keep your fingers crossed that we are able to raise the necessary funds to see this through post-production. They plan to have the final cut done by spring. I believe it will be an important film for schools and prisons alike. Everyone will be able to relate to Jimmy's compelling life story as well as his message of hope.*

And so it seems that Gino has been thinking a great deal about his skills and what his life will be like when he is released in 2016 at almost 50 years of age. I recently acquired a copy of the chapbook that Jimmy Baca published while he was in prison. In it, he shares a piece he wrote just months before his release from prison in June of 1978. *Thoughts on Leaving Prison* appears below in its entirety.

My last two months in prison have seen fourteen stabbings, three fatal and the rest deformed for life, two badly busted heads split open with pipes, and five escapes all captured shortly after their attempts. I suppose, in watching TV and reading magazines, there are still a few Custer-like criminologists, Skinnerian/Stalinist penologists, and lamb-of-god legislators, toasting such blood-thirsty results.

Frankly, from days in juvenile homes, county jails and prisons, the party has grown stale and the lie exhausted to its most probable boundaries. Those who continue to uphold that prison rehabilitates, I can only and truthfully conclude, are utterly mad.

The buildings of such institutions are Hollywood props, dividing dark ages from twentieth century. Behind them, the dark ages crack from their shell, the mold of reality we've known ceases to develop, and we find ourselves in a dark land, constructed of stone and steel, held intact with clubs, chains, dungeons, lawless tyranny, cages, ruthless torture, etc.

The hue and cry of the audience demand satiation. And with caesarian vengeance and pathos, producers and directors of the show wash their hands clean of the blood. The blood is mopped up from granite floors, the guts wiped off the bars, a nameless man or woman is buried. And the show goes on.

In childhood, shock treatments received from laws meant to be fair and equitable, left my senses charred. Twenty years later, I'm still on the trail, and find myself in prison again. I'm on the last stretch of my sentence here.

I think back on my life, as always, reflecting and reflecting just before release. Voices in me complain, curse, and are frightened. Is there something unique in me, and can I find it and build from it, a worthwhile life for myself? I found something this time around, quite beautiful and enduring: poetry.

Thoughts of my past life leave me wounded, helpless, and seem to blend with this cold, early, winter morning. I live with them, in them, and through them, and breathe the fresh air of their insights and their cold pain. But they subside, almost leave and I go on living.

Keep living in this prison, quartered in this dorm. Great granite pillars stagger ten feet apart down the middle of bunks. The dorm's split in half by a space in between where a guard regularly paces, spying both sides, where men play cards, watch TV, read, talk, or sleep. The dorm is roughly set about seven feet in the earth, so when looking out the barred windows, at the main yard gun towers, other squat cellblocks, sunset shadows spreading over the compound, guards crossing the yard, your eyelevel meets ground level.

In these closing days of my sentence, at night, when everyone sleeps, I listen to the silence ventilated by snores, coughs and farts from the men. But gradually all noise stops, and the silence swells sweetly, filling this underground home of ours. Perhaps you hear the patter of water drops from the shower stalls in the back, or someone gets up to take a piss and you can hear the creak of the steel bunk under his shifting weight, but these noises are swallowed in silence.

Someone lights a cigarette in the dark. Another old timer huddles under his home-made night lamp rolling state tobacco. I feel their presence and my own, groping like fingers on a hot stove.

I realize that just surviving has hardened me tough as plaster. And I mourn this, because to be human and feel is the greatest fortune the heart can have. Still, it takes a hammer and chisel to chip away my stolid face and locate the sensitive designs of my nature. I've barred myself up to keep the wolves from attacking, the snakes from entering, the bears from plunder in the few remaining private shrubs of fruit I have left. I've kept myself from myself so long, I've died. Being dead, you don't feel the humiliation and brutality of these cemeteries.

But it's a lie. I feel them. I stir from my grave with hunger and cold blooded instinct for human companionship and respect.

My feelings rise like ghosts and prowl the length of this midnight gallery. For years I've shared only the air with other people. People have always wanted to see "him," and not "me." And the "me" is buried underneath, a faceless, nameless me, who weeps at the destruction and sacrifice of his life, but who will not give up.

He takes the flashing shadows and gleams of light in my memory bank, and excavates them until he finds some crusty tooth of truth or some minute particle of primitive meaning, that he can use to bite into life again. And taste it!

So with these shadows and gleams of light, I've wattled a niche for myself. Here I can be free. Though all the regulations of this prison seek to string me up, cut me apart piece by piece to their liking, I don't let them.

I don't know if I am good or bad at living my life. Now at the precipice of my prison term, I look down into freedom and am shaken to the rims of myself at the wilderness that confronts and challenges me.

From the brute mammoth world of prison, where I found my strengths, shortcomings and ideals, and for them screamed, got stabbed, grew mean and fought and wept and disobeyed orders; I realize I haven't been trained, educated, or adequately prepared to push buttons and responsibly pay rent and taxes, or shake hands with policemen.

All I do passably is write poetry and stand against things I don't like. I'm as stubborn as a log. I won't survive out there with my poetry. Yet, it's almost all I know and love to do.

My poetry has warmed so cold distant worlds and suffering deep in me, as only the light of poetry can with its hope and freedom encircling the world these days. I've endangered the existence of all prisons with my blood and tears, and fed the roots of self-expression and freedom.

Jimmy's powerful last line echoed in my head long after I read it, and it spawned the title of this book you hold in your hand. It moved me to become involved with the Capital Region Ex-offender Support Coalition (CRESC) whose mission is to assist men and women with the transition from prison to the community. It nudged me to attend my first meeting of the Pennsylvania Prison Society and to become an Official Visitor and Co-Convener of the Dauphin Chapter. It compelled me to read Robert Perkinson's *Texas Tough* to begin to understand the history of penology in the United States. I hadn't read such engaging history since I read Paul Fussell's *The Great War and Modern Memory* as a humanities undergraduate student. Perkinson manages to convey a terrible history in an engaging fashion.

Sadly, not much has changed since the first substantial prison was built by Spanish soldiers in St. Augustine, Florida in 1570, and that is why I am engaging in work that improves prisoner rehabilitation and reentry programs. It is my sincere hope that future generations will benefit from a reformed, more humane approach to how America treats her incarcerated citizenry. Jimmy Santiago Baca's story and his resilience will continue to fuel my journey.

From the Outside Looking In
Kym Sheehan

Writing is a way in which we reflect upon our actions, and bare our soul not only to others, but also to oneself. Oftentimes, our journeys are intertwined with that of others; call it fate, circumstance, or choice, it happens. I have viewed the penal system from the outside in, from arrest, to trial and to sentencing and thereafter. Once as a victim of abuse, and another time as the supporting spouse of one who was incarcerated for several years. Although this is in many years past, I have yet to tell the story; although this is not the venue for that.

However, I can attest to the dehumanizing treatment received by prisoners and family alike, having watched it occur, but not directly experienced it at a maximum security prison. I can attest to the positive experience of being favored by guards due to circumstances that occurred with those behind bars and how it affects family and friends who visit those inmates. It is this experience of looking from the outside in that has always made me wonder, what if…? Jimmy Santiago Baca's story begins to answer the "what if" for me.

Additionally, I have worked in schools with students who were adorned with the "ankle bracelets" of justice, who did time weekends or weeks at a time within detention centers, and who for one reason or another, were involved with the police, be it through their own actions or that of their parents. With the numbers of students in these situations it would seem that society is not doing justice and/or the system is not working if it is so full of inmates, both young and old.

We all have faults, we all have biases, we experience love and hate, joy and sadness; however, we do it through diverse lenses. Paint the picture of you through your own lens, but don't forget about the unique views of others when you shape this understanding and your portrait, the person you are or wish to become. It is my hope that the lenses provided within this text can help the reader make sense of the journey he or she is on through thoughts, words, deeds, and/or written expression. I leave you with the words of Jimmy Santiago Baca to Tucson poet Will Inman and ask you to put yourself in the picture, **"I saw a picture of you. You looked strong. You'll be OK. Eat real hot chili if your mind gets too filled up with troubles. The chili will do two things: it will make you scream—or you will realize there are worse things in the world."**

Afterword

In 2008, Jimmy Santiago Baca took a film crew and a team of researchers to participate in a writing workshop he was giving in a series of trips to a maximum security facility in the Midwest. I was blessed and privileged to be part of that team. I so often wondered how inmates find hope in the most controlled system of our society. I've heard the screams of prisoners in solitary confinement. On this trip, I was going inside for the first time to study Jimmy's teaching. We were visiting 40 women, many in for life, and many in for first or second degree murder. Jimmy knew the drill. We went through multiples levels of protective security removing layers of clothing, shoes and bags, and going through metal detection and a double-locked passage to the cafeteria, where the workshops were held. The thinking and writing exercises Jimmy led helped us break through the greatest of walls—the self-protective and invisible walls the inmates had created before we entered the room. These women were writers, and with Jimmy's examples and exercises they grew to trust us within moments of our arrival. They opened their hearts and their souls to each other and to each of us. This life-changing experience was one I will never forget and for which I will be forever grateful.

Through Jimmy's exercises, I witnessed and participated with the women in their healing process and in the development of their creativity. You see, they had endured unimaginable pain and suffering over many years. It was not unusual in the writing workshops for the women to go deep into their life stories - deeper than they had ever gone in any therapy with staff, doctors, and psycho-social experts. Writing gave them an avenue to rewind their lives, put that life in their hands, speak it out loud, share it with each other, and from there rewrite their own futures. It was not unusual for Jimmy to receive letters from family members thanking him for the hope that grew in their daughter like roses, out of concrete walls.

When I describe Jimmy's teaching method to other professionals or to community members, they often ask the same question, "Is it something other teachers can learn to do? If Jimmy is the only person who can teach this, is it a method worth studying?" The lessons and experiences of Jimmy's workshops lead to transformation. For Jimmy, becoming a writer helped him bridge two distant worlds: the worlds of prisoner and free man. In this book, Kym Sheehan and Denise VanBriggle have captured details of Jimmy's thinking and teachings in ways that allow you to support the teaching of writing in diverse instructional settings. Kym and Denise, the poet-teachers who wrote this book, have provided detailed descriptions, exercises, sample poetry, and food for thought for teachers and students in the writing process. As our world continues to change and sustainability becomes an issue, more rapidly than at any other time of our Earth's history, our students today will need to find ways to build resiliency to face the challenges of their future. Kym and Denise dig deep into aspects rarely addressed in the writing classroom, to help students heal through self-expression, moving themselves into the worlds of freedom and creativity.

At a time when teaching beyond the test is being challenged by national standards that are confusing, high-stakes testing that is overwhelming, and crazy reforms, we want teachers to know how much we appreciate the wonderful work you do in your classrooms, workshops, and teaching. In my work preparing teachers, I often find that working out my own examples for exercises helps me better teach the process and also gives me a better understanding of the potential for what students will learn from the experience. Kym and Denise provide tremendous support for the type of writing Jimmy teaches in his workshops. As you become comfortable and more familiar with the material, I encourage you to be creative and take advantage of the events that come up in the lives of your students. Writing as a form of liberation is a process. Now that you have read the book and worked through some of the exercises, I am certain you will have your own stories to share about the power of transformational writing.

Diane Torres-Velásquez, Ph.D.
University of New Mexico

About the Authors

Jimmy Santiago Baca

Jimmy Santiago Baca was born in Santa Fe, New Mexico. Raised by his grandmother and later sent to an orphanage, he became a runaway by age 13. It was after Baca was sentenced to five years in a maximum security prison that he made literacy his focus and learned to read and write. He continually uses his gift of writing and the power of words to help others. Email: www.Cedartreepoetics.org

Jimmy was featured on Bill Moyer's Language of Life series and is the author of *A Place to Stand*, winner of The International Prize, *Martin & Meditations on the South Valley*, winner of the American Book Award, *Working in the Dark*, winner of the Southwest Book Award, and writer and executive producer of *Blood In/Blood Out*, a Hollywood Pictures feature that has gained a cult-status following of millions globally. His book *Healing Earthquakes* was an honoree of Phi Beta Kappa Society and was also the recipient of a Pushcart Prize, The Hispanic Heritage Award for Literature, and the Cornelius P. Turner Award (which honors GED graduates who have made "outstanding contributions" in areas such as education, justice, and social welfare). He was honored with the Humanitarian Award, Albuquerque, and has held many Chairs of Distinction, including The Endowed Hulbert Chair (Colorado College), the Wallace Stevens Chair (Yale), and the Berkeley Regents Chair, and was a Barnes and Noble Discover Author. After writing a Mexican Roots series for HBO, he established his nonprofit Cedar Tree, Inc., and produced two documentaries, *Lost Voices* and *Moving the River Back Home*. Cedar Tree continues to grow and assist communities through its bookmobile, which supplies free books to libraries and schools on reservations, barrios, and poor inner-city educational centers, and sends interns to assist teachers in deprived or neglected rural communities that lack educational resources. For his work teaching thousands of adults and kids to read and write, the University of New Mexico awarded him an honorary Ph.D. In October, 2018, PBS will feature a documentary on his development as a poet. While continuing to write, he facilitates writing workshops worldwide, annually visiting dozens of prisons, youth offender facilities, and alternative schools for at-risk youth in as many countries. He's the author of 18 books in print. They include:

Grove:
A Place to Stand
Healing Earthquakes
A Glass of Water
Singing at the Gates
The Importance of a Piece of Paper
C-Train, Thirteen Mexicans

New Directions:
Poemas Selectos/Selected Poems
Black Mesa Poems
Martin & Meditations on the South Valley
Immigrants in Our Own Land
Spring Poems Along the Rio Grande
Winter Poems Along The Rio Grande

Heinemann Publishers:
Stories from the Edge
Adolescents on the Edge: Stories and Lessons
To Transform Learning
(with ReLeah Lent)

Teachers College Press:
Feeding the Roots of Self-Expression and Freedom
(with Kym Sheehan and Denise VanBriggle)

Museum of New Mexico Press:
Working in the Dark

Sherman Asher Press:
The Lucia Poems
The Esai Poems

Restless Books (ebooks):
The Esai Poems
The Lucia Poems

Beacon Press:
When I Walk Through That Door, I Am (An Immigrant Mother's Quest)

Kym Sheehan

Kym Sheehan is an educator with classroom, curriculum, and media expertise. She is a member of the Tampa Bay Area Writing Project(T-BAWP) and is currently writing for Voices in the Middle. She is also an independent literacy consultant at the local and national levels. Her passions for reading and writing fuel her craft and are embedded in her daily responsibilities. Most importantly, Kym believes in the power of literacy to save lives. Kym has served teachers as President of Florida Council of Teachers of English (FCTE 2011-2013) and has been involved with the national group (NCTE) working with the anti-censorship committee. Throughout her life's journey she continues to find ways to feed her passions and promote literacy. Email: Kym_LiteracyRX@comcast.net

Denise VanBriggle

Denise VanBriggle, K-University literacy professional, National Writing Project teacher-consultant, spends most days exploring the power of various expressive arts to act as change agents, perspective shifters, and resilience builders in her own life and the lives of others. She currently serves as an official prison visitor and former Co-convener of the Dauphin County Chapter of the Pennsylvania Prison Society and owns Cityscape Consulting, a small business devoted to designing curriculum and programming to meet the unique needs of diverse clients. She is working on a collection of poetry titled *Love, Loss, and Longing.* Email: Cityscape8@gmail.com

How to Get Involved

If after reading and engaging with the poems and activities in this collection you feel moved to action and would like to get involved at the local, state, or national levels, we provide a list of suggestions and organizations you may find helpful as you make your own path.

To get involved at the local level, find your state's literacy council, prison society, and/or organization dedicated to the support prisoners' re-entry after release.

The following national and/or international organizations advocate for social justice and literacy. This list is not all inclusive; however, it serves as a beginning.

American Civil Liberties Union (ACLU)
125 Broad Street, 18th Floor
New York, NY 10004
Phone: (212) 549-2500
Website: www.aclu.org

Amnesty International
5 Penn Plaza
New York, NY 10001
Phone: (212) 807-8400
Website: www.amnestyusa.org

Get Lit
142 N. Hayworth Ave.
Los Angeles, CA 90048
Phone: (323) 930-0857
Website: www.getlit.org

Human Rights Watch
350 5th Avenue, 34th Floor
New York, NY 10118-3299
Phone: (212) 290-4700; (212) 736-1300 fax
Website: www.hrw.org

Innocence Project

40 Worth St., Suite 701

New York, NY 10013

Phone: (212) 364-5340

Website: www.innocenceproject.org

International Reading Association

800 Barksdale Rd.

PO Box 8139

Newark, DE 19714-8139

Phone: (800) 336-7323

Website: www.reading.org

National Coalition for Literacy

PO Box 2932

Washington, DC 20013-2932

Website: www.national-coalition-literacy.org

National Council of Teachers of English

1111 W. Kenyon Road

Urbana, IL 61801-1096

Phone: (217) 328-3870 or (877) 369-6283

Website: www.ncte.org

National Writing Project

University of California

2105 Bancroft Way #1042

Berkeley, CA 94720-1042

Phone: (510) 642-0963

Website: www.nwp.org

Prison Activist Resource Center

387 17th St.

Oakland, CA 94612

Phone: (510) 893-4648

Website: www.prisonactivist.org

Prison Mindfulness Institute

Integral Transformative Justice
11 S. Angell St. #303
Providence, RI 02906
Website: www.prisonmindfulness.org

Penal Reform International

60-62 Commercial Street
London E1 6LT
United Kingdom
Phone: +44 20 7924 6515; +44 20 7377 8711fax
E-mail: info@penalreform.org
Website: www.penalreform.org

Prison Fellowship Ministries

P.O. Box 17434
Washington, DC 20041
Phone: (703) 481-0000; (703) 481-0003 fax
E-mail: info@pfi.org

The Sentencing Project

1705 DeSales Street, NW
8th Floor
Washington, DC 20036
Phone: (202) 628-0871
Website: www.sentencingproject.org

Please don't forget to also be involved in your local school systems to help those in need and support all who wish to be involved in social issues.

Cited References

Baca, J. (1978). Rockbook 3. Unspecified. ASIN:B000UD8PNG

Baca, J. (1992). Coming into Language. *Working in the Dark: Reflections of a Poet of the Barrio.* Santa Fe, NM: Red Crane Books.

Baca, J. (2013). Making the Rounds. *Open the Door: Exciting Young People About Poetry.* National Poetry Foundation.

Gallagher, K. (2004). *Deeper Reading: Comprehending Challenging Texts, 4-12.* Portland, ME: Stenhouse Publishers.

Reubens, P. (Painter). (c. 1625). Judgment of Paris. [Landscape].

Turner, W. (2011). Personal correspondence from Gino.

Photograph Credits

 All tree photos obtained from Shutterstock.com

 Jimmy Santiago Baca photographed by Esai James Baca

Kym Sheehan photographed by Darrell Lupo

Denise VanBriggle photographed by Erika L. Dupes/Bliss Images

Also by Jimmy Santiago Baca

Memoir and Essays

Working in the Dark: Reflections of a Poet of the Barrio
A Place to Stand
Adolescents on the Edge
Stories from the Edge

Fiction

The Importance of a Piece of Paper
A Glass of Water

Poetry

Breaking Bread with the Darkness: Book 1—The Esai Poems
Breaking Bread with the Darkness: Book 2—The Lucia Poems
Immigrants in Our Own Land
Black Mesa Poems
Martin and Meditations on the South Valley
Healing Earthquakes
C-Train and Thirteen Mexicans
Winter Poems Along the Rio Grande
Spring Poems Along the Rio Grande
Que Linda la Brisa
Selected Poems (bilingual)
Singing at the Gates
The Face

Coming in 2019

When I Walk Through That Door, I Am (An Immigrant Mother's Quest)